D0384579

CALGARY PUBLIC LIBRARY

SEP ___ 2011

Seeing Ezra

A MOTHER'S STORY OF AUTISM, UNCONDITIONAL LOVE, AND THE MEANING OF NORMAL

Kerry Cohen

SEAL PRESS

Seeing Ezra
A Mother's Story of Autism, Unconditional Love, and the Meaning of Normal

Copyright © 2011 by Kerry Cohen

Portions of this book have been previously published in *My Baby Rides the Short Bus, McSweeney's, Portland Monthly Magazine,* and on Babble.com and Literary-Mama.com

Published by
Seal Press
A Member of the Perseus Books Group
1700 Fourth Street
Berkeley, California

All rights reserved. No part of this book may be reproduced or transmitted in any form without written permission from the publisher, except by reviewers who may quote brief excerpts in connection with a review.

Library of Congress Cataloging-in-Publication Data

Cohen, Kerry.
  Seeing Ezra : a mother's story of autism, unconditional love, and the meaning of normal / by Kerry Cohen.
    p. cm.
  Summary: "Seeing Ezra is a memoir about a mother's challenges while raising a child with autism"— Provided by publisher.
  Includes bibliographical references and index.
  ISBN-13: 978-1-58005-369-3 (hardback)
  ISBN-10: 1-58005-369-6 (hardback)
  1. Cohen, Ezra—Mental health. 2. Cohen, Kerry. 3. Autistic children—United States—Biography. 4. Parents of autistic children—United States—Biography. 5. Autistic children—Family relationships—United States. 6. Autistic children—Rehabilitation—United States. I. Title.
  RJ506.A9C626 2011
  616.85'8820092--dc22
                            2011009415

9 8 7 6 5 4 3 2 1

Cover and interior design by Domini Dragoone
Printed in the United States of America
Distributed by Publishers Group West

The author has changed some names and personal details to protect the privacy of those mentioned in the book.

For Michael, Griffin, and especially Ezra

Contents

Seeing comes before words.

—John Berger

A Note About Terminology

Throughout this book, *Seeing Ezra,* I use the term "autistic" as an adjective much more than I do as a noun. "Autism" as a noun is the more politically correct people-first language, e.g., people who have autism. People-first language originated with Kathie Snow's teaching article "People-First Language," which can be found on her website: www.disabilityisnatural.com. Snow's intention is to provide a respectful manner of writing and talking about people with disabilities by naming the people first and their disability second. She notes in the original article, "Words are powerful."

She writes:

People-first language puts the person before the disability, and describes what a person has, not who a person is.

Are you myopic or do you wear glasses?

Are you cancerous or do you have cancer?

Are you handicapped/disabled or do you have a disability?

If people with disabilities are to be included in all aspects of society, and if they're to be respected and valued as our fellow citizens, we must stop using language that marginalizes and sets them apart. History tells us that the first way to devalue a person is through language.

Words are, indeed, powerful. But rather than agree with Snow, members of the neurodiversity movement take issue with people-first language as it applies to autism. Many autistic adults note that autism is not a disease, not something separate from who they are.

Jim Sinclair, an autism rights activist and cofounder of Autism Network International, wrote "Why I Dislike 'Person First' Language," an entry that can be found in his blog at http://replay.web. archive.org/20090210190652/http://web.syr.edu/~jisincla/person_first.htm:

Saying "person with autism" suggests that the autism can be separated from the person. But this is not the case. I can be separated from things that are not part of me, and I am still the same person. I am usually a "person with a purple shirt," but I could also be a "person with a blue shirt" one day, and a "person with a yellow shirt" the next day, and I would still be the same person, because my clothing is not part of me. But autism is part of me. Autism is hard-wired into the ways my brain works. I am autistic because I cannot be separated from how my brain works.

I believe Ezra cannot be separated from his autism. I believe his autism is the same as his neurology and his neurology is *him*. Therefore, I follow Sinclair's line of reasoning for why I use the term "autistic" mostly as an adjective to describe the fundamentals of who Ezra is. He is autistic. He is also a boy. He is also funny and kind and loving and smart and talented. But I don't believe he has a disease or even some sort of disorder, even though being autistic means he is and always will be classified as such by the medical community.

Preface

I WANT YOU to see Ezra, his straw-colored hair, his soft pink cheeks. He twirls and dances through the world, laughing, humming. I am afraid I don't have the language to describe him the right way. Do you see him? How he smiles slyly, how he sees you looking, how he hears everything and sometimes nothing. How he is just a child, like any other child, and also how he is different. How he is so much more, always, than you think he might be.

Right now there is something he wants. This is unusual. More often, he needs nothing. He just plays. He looks through books. He plays on the computer. He says a word to his brother, Griffin, who wants most to thrill Ezra. Griffin performs for him while Ezra laughs. We all feel like Griffin does. We all want so much for Ezra to be with us at every moment, to see us: Look at me, Ezra! Look!

Look! He does, but he doesn't need us, not at all the way we need him. The three of us—Griffin, their father, Michael, and I—we follow Ezra, reaching for him, desperate in our love. Our wants are so big, so thick and aching. We want him, we want connection, we want nothing we know how to name.

Ezra hugs and kisses us, he smiles, he gazes with affection. He doles out his love in necessary amounts. Who is this child whom I could not live without? He is fuller, more whole, than anyone I've known. His teachers and therapists spend endless amounts of energy trying to make him want more, but I am secretly envious of his self-containment.

But now he wants something. His want is simple. He wants more milk. As usual, I've complicated things. I've brought in my own mundane and silly wants, which are always, always in the way. I want him to answer yes, such a simple little word. He has said it before. He's been talking for two and a half years now, but for reasons known only to him, he refuses to use this word. He will say okay. He will say no. He'll say any number of the thousands of words he knows. But he will not say yes.

So, right now, after he's asked me for milk and I'm sure I've heard him right, I say, "What was that, Ezra? You say you want milk?"

And he answers, "Milk," as usual.

"Say yes," I tell him.

"I want milk."

"Say yes, and I'll give you milk."

"I want milk," he says again, with stronger inflection.

At this point, obviously, yes is irrelevant. Our conversations, if you can call them that, always reach this point. I know what he wants. He knows I know what he wants. But now I've got it in my head that he has to say yes, that he has to use the language I want him to use. It is one of the many dances Ezra and I go through. He does this same dance with his dad. We become determined that Ezra do something that is outside his natural comfort zone and that is clearly pointless or disconcerting to him, and he gets irritated. I fear I don't see him enough, or I see him wrongly, or I simply don't know how to see. It is so difficult, this business of seeing.

Caught up now, forgetting to see him, I come up with a new tactic. He knows how to read and spell. Words and letters endlessly fascinate him. Why not use that? "Y-e-s," I say. "What's that spell?"

"Whys," he answers, verbalizing the phonetic spelling of the letters.

I frown. "No, Ezra, not *whys*. Y-e-s."

"Whys," he says again, but then his face breaks into a smile. He hears it, the joke, the triumph. He knows what y-e-s spells, but it might also be the plural of *y*. Many *ys*. "*Whys*." He erupts into laughter.

Oh, I wish you could see him, the way his eyes are like prisms of lights, the way the whole world goes silent when he laughs, everything listening, listening.

"Ezra," I say. I'm smiling now, too, impossible not to when he laughs like this. But my want is still there. It still tugs at me, trying to manipulate him to say the right word. "Tell me what y-e-s spells."

"*Whys!*" He can barely get it out, he's laughing so hard. "Y-e-s! Whys!"

I can't help it. Finally I break into laughter with him, giving in to him and his world. Why does it take me so long, when we are both so much happier here, in this middle place? We say the non-word together again and again. "Whys, whys, whys!"

Fall in Oregon

TWO YEARS OLD

Mind Blindness

The first time I hear the word "autism" associated with my son, he is only a year old, and it comes from his young baby sitter. She is a nice girl, a little awkward, who seems to love Ezra from the start. She shows that she is interested in gaining my approval, glancing at me often, watching for my reaction to whatever she says and does. This is fine with me since she's caring for my baby. But somewhere along the way, after about three months, things start heading south. For one, she and her husband have been trying to become pregnant for over a year and nothing is happening. Her desperation about it bothers me, reminiscent actually of my own frantic need for a baby before Ezra was born. She talks about it a lot, too much. Little things also begin to slip into conversation: Her husband doesn't like her to be out by herself, away from where he can protect her; and she's struggled with depression in the past, has been stable on meds, but now isn't taking them anymore.

I start to feel uncomfortable, and feeling uncomfortable about the person taking care of my child is not an option. I ask her to come by one day when she isn't working, and I tell her I need to let her go. She cries. She says she understands, but she's so sorry and she hopes I don't think badly of her. I tell her I don't. We sit for a good hour, her crying, me appeasing, until finally she seems ready to go. As we approach the door, she turns to me.

"One thing I want to be sure to say," she starts, "because I wouldn't be able to forgive myself if I didn't."

I wait. I have no sense of the huge thing she's about to say, no sense that life will forever be altered.

"I think Ezra's on the autistic spectrum," she states. Here's what happens to me in this moment: An electric bolt shoots through my body. I think *Rain Man*. Institutions. Mental retardation. Rocking. Wordless. Empty. Alone. I think, *Please God, no.* She lists a couple reasons she believes this. She says Ezra has a tendency to be very involved with something, and that he doesn't look at her unless she's singing. He's picky about eating. He stays very focused on whatever toy he's playing with. He doesn't seem to understand much of what she says.

Do I know these things? Yes, yes, of course I do. He's my child. I have been with him since the beginning, have held him close to me, inside me, since he was a drop of possibility. At seven weeks

two years old

pregnant, in a therapy session during which I was afraid because of a previous miscarriage, I closed my eyes, quieted myself, and felt him inside my body: a whole person, a whole separate being who was not me, for whom I was simply a vessel. I know every inch of him, the beauty mark on his belly, the way his skin turns red when he's upset. I know these observations that this girl has made about my son, and yet they've never caused me concern. Not even an ounce. He's a happy baby. A loving, affectionate baby. He *is* engaged—you just have to know how to engage him. So he loves music. So what? As for his understanding what someone else is saying, well, he's only a year old. Surely, he'll catch up.

I return to that moment again and again, holding it in my hand like an iridescent shell, turning it this way and that, trying to understand, trying to reconcile the anger that rises up as I do. Because that one small exchange effectively ended my innocence as a mother. From that day on, until he was around four years old, I couldn't see my little boy clearly. He grew blurry, far away. Everything became cause for evaluation. I constantly asked: *Was that a normal thing to do? Should he be doing it another way?* I examined other children his age and wondered how they were different, how my child was maybe not right. I lost sight of him, my small, precious, beautiful blond love, and to this day I feel furious about it. I want to claim that time back. I want to go back to that moment when she said, "One thing I want to be sure to say," and exclaim, "No, say nothing," and push her more quickly out the door. I want to never have hired her at all.

Eventually, I would have noticed that Ezra's development was different, sure. In time, I would have worried enough about his eating to seek help. But my right to that process, my right to my son, was stolen from me. My entire story as Ezra's mother is, in some ways, defined by this moment. I would never be the same. My family could never be the same. Ezra's autism changed us, yes. But so did this moment. It held inside it everything that has been harmful to us about Ezra's autism. *He* is fine. His autism, even, is fine. But how hard it was at this time to know my child, how difficult it was to understand what his autism meant to me, to our family, to him—how long it took to settle into and arrive at that understanding because this babysitter's words took me off my own instinctual track—that has been more painful to me than almost anything else as Ezra's mother.

When I hear people now tell their righteous, heroic stories of letting parents know they see something concerning in another person's child, that old rage comes back. When they claim other parents are in denial, I want to scream, *How dare you! How dare you think you know what other people need, what they know and don't know about their children! How dare you take their process of discovery from them!* Some may argue the earlier a child is provided services, the better. The sooner you send them to therapies and programs, the sooner they will change. I don't buy it. I don't believe in the small-window-of-time theory any more than I believe that all parents need to be anxious to change how their children interact with the world. Any more than I believe a child with autism can stop being autistic through therapy, or that autistic people don't come to their own understandings once they are ready, regardless of therapies, just on a different timeline from others.

More important, perhaps, I don't buy that knowing your child is autistic at one year old—which is the new push from the American Pediatric Association—is more useful than the ways in which a family will suffer, and never on their own terms. Because will it be okay with them, with the APA, with their communities and schools, if their child doesn't improve through therapies? Will it be okay if—even after a lot of therapy—that child can't function in a classroom meant for neurotypical children?

Nobody seems to think about the harm that can come to a family, to a child, from pushing them into the world all special needs families must enter, one full of evaluations and interventions and schedules and do something fast now—quick, or else. No one considers that a family might do better, might have enough where-withal even, to make its own choices about what's right for it, but not necessarily for everyone else. The overwhelming pressure to follow proven scientific guidelines about early intervention often steals parents' courage to follow their instincts and blinds them to their baby as just that, a baby. No one considers that, while yes, you *do* make choices for your child when you are ready, if that happens at two or three, that child will still do as well as he would have had you caught it six months earlier. This isn't cancer, after all, with cells that will grow and spread. This is a neurological difference. A difference that will not ever become as not different as those early-intervention pushers seem to want everyone to believe.

But I'm getting ahead of myself, because the day that baby sitter said the words "autistic spectrum" to me, I'm not there yet. I'm suddenly not anywhere. I'm knocked off the world I thought I knew. It will be a long time before I feel this anger, a long time before I understand what was done to my family, what is mandatory experience for all families with a special need. For now, I am singly, unbearably terrified. For now, I am too scared to move.

Once Ezra is asleep, I go online, my stomach hollow and aching, my body alive and pinging with fear—fear of the only notion I have about autism: that it will destroy my son. This night brings the beginning of everything I will come to know about autism, just the tip of a beginning. This is the first day of what will quickly become the rest of my life. The day autism throws open the door of my house, the doorknob banging against the back wall. The day autism begins weaving its way through my every moment, standing at my shoulder while I'm on the phone with a friend, while I'm buttering toast, while I'm brushing my teeth, having sex with my husband. Tonight, autism comes into my house and settles into the cushions of my couch. As of tonight, autism is here to stay. It will not be leaving, not ever again, and tonight that idea terrifies me.

I type "autism" into my search engine and learn that it is caused by so many possibilities that I can't separate them in my head. It's caused by so many possibilities that they all seem to negate the last

two years old

possibility: *genetics ... vaccinations ... Candida ... leaky gut ... gluten ... birth trauma ... mercury ... heavy metals ... dental amalgams ... breastfeeding ... bottle feeding ... allergies ... immunity functions ... television.* I leave this information alone for now. I don't go down the what-did-I-do-to-cause-this path, because for now I'm not convinced anything is wrong. But I file awareness that the reason matters. It matters hugely that I know *why.* That I find someone to blame, even if more often than not that someone will be myself.

In one of the child psychology courses I took to become a psychotherapist, I learned the abstract facts about autism: Autism is defined by communication delays, social delays, and repetitive behaviors. Autism is, essentially, a constellation of symptoms. I learned about autism only as a severe affliction, one that would never alter in the course of a person's life. I learned about autism as a catastrophe. I try to see myself as a student, taking neat notes during the lecture. Ezra was already growing in my belly, a little fish, twisting and waving, becoming.

Tonight, I learn about autism from a parent's perspective: the red flags that include not pointing or waving by twelve months, neither of which Ezra does. He hasn't adopted any of the sign language I've been diligently trying to teach him since he was nine months old—a vestige of my good-parenting plan I created before he was born. He cries when a music CD ends, wanting it to play again and again.

But there's so much I read about autism that doesn't fit Ezra. He has normal eye contact, at least once he is comfortable with someone.

He initiates peekaboo and chasing games. He plays normally with most toys, albeit sometimes in rigid ways. He engages us as long as what we are doing interests him. He's affectionate and doesn't mind loud noises or sudden changes or if we want to join him in his play or mess with what he's already doing. He's one year old, a baby still. It's so hard to know. Children can be weird. Children can develop at different rates. They can do things you don't expect.

I interview new babysitters, asking them, "How do you deal with toddlers who are different from other children?" They bite their lips, look at their hands. They don't know how to answer my odd question. One says, "I don't know. The same way I'd deal with any toddler?" This is the one I hire.

At eighteen months Ezra learns sign language for "more." I have been trying to teach him for the better part of a year, pushing my fingertips against each other again and again, saying, *"More, Ezra. Look at my hands. More, more."* We're in New Seasons, a natural-food store. We're surrounded by parents of children who learned sign language when they should have, who feed their children only organic yogurt and fresh vegetables because their children will eat these things. Ezra is in his stroller and I'm handing him one cheese puff at a time, urging him to ask for more. He looks at the bag, leans toward it, says, *"Mm mm mm."* Finally, he does it. He presses his chubby dimpled hands together. He watches them as he does. "More!" I yell. "You signed 'more'!" I hand him the puff and he sticks it in his mouth, unfazed.

two years old

I tell Michael that evening and he lights up. He hasn't been burdened by my fears. Not yet. He heard the word "autism" and waved his hand dismissively. "No way," he said. He and Ezra play intensely. Michael chases him while Ezra squeals. He throws Ezra into the air and catches him. They have set games: Michael says, "Get out of here. Go on." And Ezra starts to walk away. Then Michael grabs Ezra's shirt and says, "Get back here," and they erupt into giggles.

Early Intervention

When Ezra is almost two years old, he still isn't consistent with sign language and he has no words, so I think about pursuing outside opinions. I call Early Intervention first, a state program that is mandated by federal law. From zero to three years of age, every child is entitled to have a governmental service agency perform developmental evaluations and provide services. The local Early Intervention program is tied into the Portland educational system, the idea being that a child can receive help early on, and then, when he enters school at three, will continue receiving those services through the school.

"What sorts of things are you concerned about?" the coordinator asks me on the phone.

"I'm not *concerned*," I say. I'm aware I'm pacing as we talk. "But I know he's supposed to have a few words by now, and I figure speech therapy could help."

"So, he isn't talking yet. How old is he, again?"

I tell her, not wanting to. He's twenty-one months.

"Any other concerns?"

His poor eating. No pointing. Crying when songs end. He cries in terrible despair if someone sings one of his favorite songs.

"No," I say. "No. Just the words."

We set a date and time, and I immediately start to dread the coming appointment. In moments, I am stricken with instinctual fear. What have I done? Allowing others to get their sticky something-is-wrong-with-your-son hands on my boy? Somehow I know that the moment they walk into our house, things will be out of hand. Somehow I understand they will take my son and grip him in their claws, in their estimation of who he is, based on his imperfections. Somehow I intuit that I will have to scramble to keep him safe, to try to hold on to him. That our lives are about to irrevocably change.

The day of the evaluation, Ezra is in a good mood. He has gotten a good night's sleep. Has been playing all morning. The team—a lead evaluator (whom I spoke with on the phone), a pregnant speech therapist, and an occupational therapist—marches into the house with a bag full of toys and eyes Ezra. My heart batters against my chest. I know they're here to evaluate him. I'm not an idiot. But every bit of me doesn't want it. I know they will examine my child as though he were bacteria in a petri dish, and short of making them leave, I won't be able to stop it. I want him to receive speech therapy,

I remind myself. I want him to have the chance to catch up. Unfortunately, this is what we must endure.

Almost as if Ezra knows what they are here for, almost like he intends to shake things up, get this party started, he flips over a toy car and spins its wheels—a classic autism move. And something he has never ever done before. *Boom!*

"Is this something he does often?" the lead asks.

"He's never done that before in his life," I say. They watch him, excited.

"As far as you know," the pregnant one corrects.

I shoot a look her way. What is that supposed to mean? I already don't like her. I don't like the way she glanced around my house after they were settled in, evaluating not just Ezra, apparently, but my decorating. I don't like that she asked to use the bathroom, pointing to her belly, and when she came out said, "Those are the same colors we're painting our nursery." I don't like that she's caught up in thinking about herself. More than that, something about the way she referred to her precious belly but then looked at Ezra like he was diseased makes me certain she believes herself immune to the possibility of having a child with special needs herself. Advanced educational degrees don't transform people into superhumans, after all. Anyone can birth a child with special needs.

Next, the lead evaluator begins with the questions, questions I will hear often during the next couple years, questions I will answer again and again:

Tell me about your pregnancy with Ezra. It was good, easy.

Any excessive nausea? Any medication? Any smoking? Drinking? Drug use? No. No. No. No. No.

Does he tantrum? Um, sometimes. He's one (or two or three). Don't all one-year-olds (or two-year-olds or three-year-olds) tantrum?

Does he cry when you take a toy from him? I suppose so. I don't generally take his toys away from him.

What sorts of toys does he like most? Books, cars, trains, contraptions that drop balls. Is that okay?

Does he play with these toys in odd ways? No. Odd ways? No, I don't think so.

Does he cry when he wakes up from naps? Yes, sometimes.

He doesn't say "Mama" when he wants you to come to him? No. He has no words.

Does he like to spin around? Yes, of course. Don't all children?

When he spins, does he grow dizzy? I think so.

But you don't know for sure? I guess not, no.

Meanwhile, one of the evaluators, the occupational therapist, is busy with Ezra. I keep looking over nervously, seeing Ezra grow frustrated each time she shows him a toy, tells him how to play with it, watches him play with it for a few moments in his own way, and then takes it away. She wears that same quizzical, analytical look, the one all evaluators are apparently required to wear. By the time a half hour has passed, Ezra is fully upset. He runs toward me, sobbing.

"Mama!" he calls, although I'm pretty sure it's just word sounds he makes when upset.

"I see he says 'Mama,'" the lead evaluator says without emotion, while Ezra clings to me. She jots this into her notebook.

I hold him, his small, soft body, and nod, wanting Ezra to gain this one positive mark today. When they finally leave, I put Ezra down for his nap, and then I sit on the couch and cry. I call Michael.

"You don't know how they look at him," I tell him. "Like he's not even a person. He's just a baby."

"Then why are we doing this?" he asks.

"I'm supposed to," I explain. "To be a good mom, I have to help him."

I have to pull myself together. I have to be stronger, more resilient. I have to be a better mom. We have another evaluation coming up in just a couple months, this one with a private hospital's rehabilitation center, which is covered by our insurance. I want Ezra to receive as much speech therapy as possible. I'm certain he'll qualify for services with Early Intervention, but they warned me early on that their budget rarely allows for therapy more often than every other week. I wish we could just ask for speech therapy and receive it as easily as I can the antibiotics pediatricians prescribe when I say my kid is sick. I wish I could interview the evaluators, not the other way around. I wish I could just tell them yes, he's behind in acquiring language, and that could be enough. That I could be trusted, as my son's mother, to know what he needs. But this isn't the way it works.

They have to determine for themselves that he needs it, and for that to happen, we have to endure more horrible evaluations.

In the waiting room of the children's rehabilitation center, I feel stupidly optimistic. I have learned nothing yet. I'm naive and gullible. I haven't yet suffered through enough specialists eyeing my child with that particular mix of scrutiny and judgment, as if he were a strange creature in a cage. I haven't yet listened to enough experts tell me that my son is disordered, that he will never do this and might always do that. I haven't yet come to know that the world will not welcome my child.

Ezra watches the fish in the aquarium. I crouch down with him and point out the different fish, modeling for him the words. "Blue fish. And there! A yellow fish. So pretty." He stares into the tank, smiling at the fish. I just found out a few weeks ago that I'm pregnant again. I'm constantly fighting nausea and fatigue. With all the concerns that have begun to bear down on us—on me—about Ezra since Early Intervention's visit, I feel uncertain about having another baby. It's not that I worry this baby will have special needs, although, based on the statistics, I probably should. I worry I don't have it in me to care as much about another human being. I fear my heart might explode once there are two.

We received a copy of Early Intervention's report a few days earlier. How can I describe what it feels like to read such a document about my son? Substandard scores, observed doing this and not doing that. How can I explain the pain? Your child—the same one who giggles, who pushes his truck along the floor, who claps and dances—he is not doing x, y, and z. He is doing w, but only about as well as 10 percent of the other kids his age. He is in the bottom percentile for this, and isn't even on the charts for that. He doesn't do v when we ask him to, which must mean he can't do v at all. He is no good. He is no good at all.

The speech pathologist leads us into a room no bigger than a closet. One toy, a ball, dirty and played with to death, lies against the wall. She shuts the door behind us.

"Hi, Ezra!" the woman says, insincere and too loud. Ezra ignores her.

"I think he's coming down with something," I say, already starting what will become a long habit of making excuses to protect him from others' judgment. She nods and writes this down, but I can tell by the way she examines Ezra that nothing is going to keep her from making whatever assumptions she's going to make.

Ezra looks around the room.

"Don't you have any toys for him to play with?" I ask.

"We take out one at a time to see what he does with them." She points to the ball and says in that same fake voice, "There's a ball, Ezra. See the ball?"

Ezra glances at the ball and goes to the door. He reaches for the knob. He's about to start crying.

"He's not into balls," I say. "Can we please take something else out for him?"

The woman looks at me evenly. "He doesn't like balls?"

I shake my head. My palms feel sweaty. "He used to," I say defensively, but it's too late. She writes down this fact that Ezra doesn't play with balls. Ezra begins to cry, and she writes this as well.

"Come here, Ez," I say. "Come have nursies."

He climbs onto my lap, sobbing, and I pull out a boob. The woman eyes us.

"Does he nurse often for comfort?"

"He still nurses, yes," I say. "From what I understand, that's a good thing."

She cocks her head, but doesn't say anything. Nervous in the silence, I go on.

"He nurses less now that I'm pregnant," I tell her. "I think my milk is starting to dry up."

Suddenly, she smiles, the first genuine smile I've seen from her, and she puts her hand on her belly. "I'm pregnant too!" she exclaims. "Four months."

Another pregnant evaluator. What luck.

She unlocks a cabinet and takes out blocks. I'm beginning to get a headache.

"You know, Ezra's not really into blocks, either," I tell her.

She gives him another analyzing stare. "He has limited play."

"No," I say. "He plays with lots of things. Just not balls and blocks." I can hear how pathetic I sound, how desperate. Ezra still tugs away on my nipple. I don't look at him, ashamed of my need to have this woman think he's good enough. "He's been putting the shapes in his shape sorter in the correct holes since he was sixteen months. And he's stacked his cups in the right order since fifteen months."

The woman nods. She wears nothing in her expression, no empathy, no emotion of any kind. She's like a robot. I have never hated anyone more.

Ezra stops nursing, more relaxed now, and she calls him over to look at the blocks. They are small, all the primary colors. To my surprise, he starts stacking them, building a little tower, saving the blue and red ones for last, like he always does.

"Blue and red, always last," I say, delighted, proud, but seeing her face, I immediately wish I'd kept my mouth shut.

"What do you mean?"

"He usually saves the blue and red pieces for last," I say quietly.

"With every toy?"

"Not *every* toy." Most every toy.

"Hmm." She stands up and scribbles that on her pad.

As soon as she does, Ezra goes to the door again and starts to whimper. I'm pretty sure he's feeling my stress, my energy pulled tight like a stretched rubber band.

She watches him as his cries turn into full-on sobs. "Have you considered PDD?" she asks me. "That stands for 'pervasive developmental disorders,'" she adds, thinking I'm some kind of moron.

I start gathering my stuff. "I know what PDD is," I say. "I thought we were here to do an evaluation for speech therapy. If I'm not mistaken, speech therapists can't diagnose."

She puts a hand over her belly, protective. I know what she's thinking. I know she, like that therapist who came to my house, believes her own body could never bring forth anything that wasn't perfect. I know she believes Ezra isn't.

"I want you to do everything you can for Ezra," she says in a calm, condescending voice, one they must teach child therapists to use with parents. "I want him to receive all the help he needs."

I want to say, *How dare you, how dare you!* But I say, "He's fine. I've got it. But thanks anyway."

Ezra is still crying, jiggling the door handle to get out.

"Lots of children look fine, but they're really not," she argues.

I wish I could formulate what I want to say, what it will take me years to know how to say: There is nothing wrong with him. He has a pretty severe speech and comprehension delay, yes. He does a lot of things differently from other kids his age. But there is nothing *wrong*. I don't have the right words yet, and even someday when I do, I will still be misunderstood. People will still assume they know better than I do what my son needs. People will still accuse me of not doing enough for my son, even though I will always seek out services, always make sure he receives the therapies he needs. I will always doubt, too, whether the services and therapies really do anything other than make him feel like he can't just be himself. Unless I hate the things that make him different from other children, I will always be considered a wayward mother.

I scoop him up and we head toward the exit.

"Thank you," I say, though I wish now I hadn't.

"Bye, Ezra," she says, and when I glance back I see the pity and disapproval on her face.

On the drive home, I call Michael, crying. "She thinks there's something wrong with him," I say.

Michael stays calm. "Based on what?"

"Because he always puts the red and blue blocks last," I say, knowing I'm making no sense. "And because he nurses for comfort still, I think." I can't remember any details now. All I see is her disapproving face.

"Kerry," he says. "Do you hear how ridiculous that is? Ezra isn't talking yet, that's all."

"Okay," I say. I grip the phone, needing his reassurance. "You're right."

"Are you going to be all right?" I hear the frustration in his voice.

"You don't know what it's like to go to these evaluations," I say. "You don't have any idea."

"Then stop doing them," he says.

A few weeks later, that report arrives in the mail. I throw it on the kitchen counter, unopened, and leave it there for a few days. I already know what's in it: more commentary about how Ezra doesn't measure up. Any kid who isn't typically developing will invariably fail a developmental test. Let's face it, if I am looking to compare a nontypically developing child with a control group of hundreds of typically developing children (which I'm not, not even then), my kid is not going to come out looking very good.

Friends say, "Boys sometimes develop later." They chase Ezra around the house while he giggles. They hide behind doors and pop out, making him laugh. Then he hides. They say, "Where's Ezra?" And he runs out, laughing. They say, "This is not an autistic child." Ezra's pediatrician says, "I bet he's going to suddenly speak in sentences someday, surprising everyone." A friend who is also a child therapist tells me, "You may have to accept that he's developmentally delayed. But he's not autistic."

Everyone has a story of a late talker. A friend's nephew didn't say anything until he was three, and then he spoke in full sentences. Another friend whose son they had started to wonder about—*Will he ever talk?*—one day opened a cupboard and said, "Where da cookies?" My mother tells me about her friend's granddaughter who had said nothing, and then right after her second birthday twirled around and around and said, "I dizzy!" I nod my head, eager for these stories, for the promises. I tell Michael the stories and he tells me the ones his coworkers have shared. We want this so badly. We want so much for this all to be a fluke, a glitch in the system. Yet a small part of me—that part I used to trust but now question relentlessly—knows it won't be.

EZRA'S NANNY QUITS because she wants to bring her toddler daughter with her while she's with Ezra. I said that was fine, but the nanny says it never is. Ezra cries when her daughter tries to play with him. She says something about how she doesn't want his behavior with her daughter to change her sociability. I hold back tears after she calls, afraid of what I imagine the future might be. It's so hard to know what matters and what doesn't matter. Her experience might just be a clash of two toddlers' personalities, but it might also mean there is something unconscionable about my son, that parents will always pull their children away from him, afraid of his influence. I don't speak a word of it to Michael. I add it instead to the ball of tangled string that has lodged itself in my throat, right above my heart.

Early Intervention sends a therapist. I requested someone other than the pregnant woman. His name is Dave. He's tall, lanky, and immensely kind. He sits down on the floor with Ezra and speaks in a soft voice. He follows Ezra around the playroom, trying to interact. Everything Ezra does, Dave beams at. "Hey, that's great, Ezra!" And then to me, "He's doing some really neat things here." Dave will only be able to come every other week, as they warned.

Someone from the private rehabilitation center calls to tell us that we've been approved for twelve sessions. I put Ezra in the car, and we drive over. As I pull into the shadowy parking structure, I glance nervously at Ezra through the rearview mirror. I'm afraid he'll recognize where we are, remember our last experience here. I park and carry him to the elevator. He seems unconcerned. Even in the waiting room, he dances happily in front of the aquarium. I'm glad he's not upset, but now I'm also worried. Shouldn't he remember our last visit? What does it mean that he doesn't?

A young woman, a girl really, calls us back, and again we find ourselves in a closet-size room with minimal toys. The girl is friendly but a little anxious. She explains that she's interning, and that we're being watched through the two-way mirror on the wall. She asserts that she's the one being judged, not Ezra. Ezra, meanwhile, has found a toy he likes—a four-level ramp to roll balls down. He takes the balls and happily sends them down, and then the speech therapist intern comes over to ruin his fun. It's what all speech therapists do to tempt him to use words, or at least communicative gestures: They attempt to frustrate him into speech. The girl does exactly that. She takes all the balls from him and holds them behind her back. Then she says, "What do you want, Ezra? Tell me." He pushes at her, trying to reach the balls. "Tell me," she says again. She shows him the sign for "ball," palms curved around each other in the shape of a ball. "Ball?" she says. "Do you want the ball?" Ezra whines. Of course he wants the ball. He tries to get at them. He can see them there. But she moves again, so he can't reach them. "Ball," she says, making the sign again.

I take a deep breath, trying to calm myself, trying to contain the immense force of my instincts that tell me to take my son away.

"Ball," she says, louder, frustrated herself. But then she remembers herself. She glances quickly at the two-way mirror and then

two years old

smiles at Ezra. He starts to cry. I go to him. I smile curtly and gather up our stuff. Therapy over. Thanks for the help. When they call again to set up a new appointment, I say no.

"I'm sorry," I whisper to Ezra in the car. "I'm sorry," I whisper to him while he nurses to sleep. "I'm sorry," I whisper when I check on him in his crib before I go to bed. I lie in bed and worry, Michael's snoring keeping me awake anyway. We have not had sex since conceiving the new baby. There are things I will not think about. One is my waning sex life with Michael. Another is Ezra's future. At this point, I have to assume autism is simply a stumbling block, something we will move through. I am entirely here and now. I am entirely consumed with this moment. I will not step forward from it. I cannot.

The next time Dave visits Ezra, I ask him if he knows of any private speech therapists. I explain to him what we've experienced so far. I tell him I want someone who will be caring and positive, the way he is with my son. He treats Ezra like a human being, which doesn't seem to come naturally for all practitioners who work with children. Dave tells me about a few therapists. He highlights one named Patti, who, he says, he would want working with his own children.

Patti and I chat first on the phone, and I like her immediately. I like that she understands my hesitation, that she laughs when I call the therapy technique "frustrating the child," and then says, "It doesn't have to be frustrating." When I bring Ezra to her office, my body tight with anxiety, Ezra actually has a good time. I notice she really does use the same approach as the other therapists, trying to encourage Ezra to communicate, but she backs off expertly at the first hint of upset. Our insurance won't cover Patti's sessions, but I set up appointments anyway for the next few months. We'll just have to figure it out.

I also have to find an occupational therapist, because I'm quickly building awareness that Ezra has issues with eating. When he sat in his high chair, a baby, I spooned into his mouth peaches, bananas, apples, rice cereal. When he began to feed himself, he pinched Cheerios between his pointer finger and thumb and pressed them past his lips. But now he won't eat anything. More accurately, he eats three things: cheese puffs (*natural* cheese puffs, I always add defensively); a very particular type of organic cookie; and pizza. While he won't put other food in his mouth, he seems happy to place dirty leaves in there. He eats sand, clay, and paper. I have seen him try to eat dead, muddy leaves. He has chewed on twigs and rubber shapes meant for dogs, and has ripped Nerf balls into various pieces of foam with his teeth. I have pulled pebbles, marbles, string, rubber bands, tissue wads, and packing peanuts from his mouth, terrified he would choke.

Eventually I'll call this what it is: pica, a childhood disorder characterized by compulsive and persistent cravings for nonfood items, such as mud and paper. Pica is common among children with autism. For now, it is one more confusing aspect of Ezra's behavior, one more thing I can't discern as a quirk or a symptom of something larger. To assist with Ezra's eating issues, Early Intervention sends us an occupational therapist once a month. She's very nice, and even seems to know how to help, but she and I both know that once-a-month therapy is useless.

Still, Ezra and I are at capacity. This is enough for now.

But I worry that it's not *really* enough, and I also worry it's too much, that the therapies are stressing his tiny, not-even-two-year-old world. I worry he isn't being allowed to just be a little kid. I worry, always, that in my inability to know either way, to know which is more important right now, I'm failing him. That I am not giving him what he needs. I worry, I worry. It's impossible not to.

Genetic Markers

When I'm thirteen weeks pregnant with my second baby, I have genetic testing done. This is a standard option for pregnant women, and is encouraged for women over thirty-five years old. It has nothing to do with Ezra or my concerns. I refused the testing offered to me when I was pregnant with Ezra, and so, knowing this will be my last baby, feeling more confident than the last time and genuinely curious, I decide to go ahead and do it. My mother, who happens to be visiting, comes with me. She's an obstetrician, so for the majority of our meeting she and the genetic counselor share statistics and thoughts while I listen. Then they do an ultrasound, where it looks like everything is normal. Finally, they take some blood.

I don't think about politics. I don't think about autism, which can't be detected through blood or ultrasound. Not yet. I don't think about the fact that organizations are already pushing research efforts to locate an autism gene, or that after I've birthed one autistic child—if indeed that's what Ezra is—my chances of having another one increase. Autism is not on the genetic counseling roster. Not yet. I don't think about the idea that someone might have told me, had the research already been done, that Ezra was going to be autistic, and that weighed only by the skewed images I had about autism, I might have made a choice . . . I still can't think about it. I can't. I can't go there, to this horrible, societal, personal truth.

Before my mother leaves, she says about Ezra, "He's so engaged, Kerry. He's fine." I smile and nod and hold him close. I dislike that I keep having to have this conversation, that I'm always anxious, that people feel they have to reassure me. I'm very aware that nothing about this concern and confusion is helpful or useful to either Ezra or me. Still, I won't have him diagnosed.

Why? You must be wondering. *Why not just find out for sure?*

Because I wouldn't believe it.

Because he's young enough that development is too variable.

Because children are diagnosed all the time, and then they grow a little older and their diagnoses change.

Because no one seems to have a clear grasp on what autism really is.

Because right now everyone and their brother is being diagnosed with autism, not always accurately, and I'd like to wait until the fury passes.

Because we don't need a diagnosis in Oregon to receive the services.

Because I'm not ready.

And maybe because I'm not strong enough to hear that he is autistic. I'm not courageous enough to bear the truth.

Right after the pregnancy testing, our new German au pair, Nadine, arrives. After all the babysitting and nanny debacles, and knowing we have another baby on the way, we decide an au pair is our best, most reliable bet. My friend, who lives back East, teases me. She says only the wealthy have au pairs (incidentally, she will have one herself in a couple years). Actually, au pairs are a great deal for nonrich people. It requires a chunk of change up front, but once an au pair moves into your house, you receive up to forty-five hours of work from her for very little cash out. They also enjoy free food and a nice place to live.

Michael drives to the airport past midnight to pick her up. We've set up her bedroom and bathroom. We've shown Ezra photos of her. We've bought the food she told us she likes to eat. Mostly, we pray this will somehow work well.

I'm asleep when Michael arrives home with her. I find out the next morning that she barely spoke. Michael and I decide she's just shy and not used to speaking English. We go through our day, aware of her closed bedroom door and the fact that she hasn't come out. Once, we hear her emerge and go to the bathroom, so we prepare to welcome her, but then she goes back to the bedroom and disappears again. Finally, around dinnertime, she comes upstairs. She is quiet, phlegmatic, with a flat expression. She answers our polite questions: the flight was good. I let her know it's okay to feel overwhelmed or like she's missing home, but she smiles politely and says she's fine, just tired. Ezra is in the playroom, so she goes to see him. She says nothing, only looks at him a moment and smiles, and then she goes back to bed.

Michael looks at me. "Shit," he says.

The next day she feels less jet-lagged, and we take her to see Portland. She sits in the back seat with Ezra and says nothing. We drive through neighborhoods and take her to a view of the city.

"It's nice," Nadine says without expression. She is unreadable.

In bed that night, Michael and I discuss the idea that hiring an au pair was a mistake. I get up and pull out the forms to see what we'd need to do to hire a new one.

The following day, I leave her for a few hours with Ezra and go to a coffee shop. I call a friend and tell her I don't think this is going to work out. When I come home, however, I find Nadine and Ezra sending balls down the ramp on his favorite toy. Ezra watches carefully as the ball descends, dropping from row to row.

two years old

They work together. Nadine says a few words here and there. "Do you want another ball, Ezra?" Their energy is calm, entwined; they are in their own soft world, and there is no question in my mind that Ezra likes it.

Ezra loves books. When he was just two months old, I sat him on my still-bloated postpartum lap and read to him. Even then, so tiny, he stared intently at the pages. At just five months, he began turning the pages himself, always waiting until I was done reading the last line. His favorite books have always been the ones with singsong rhythm, such as *Brown Bear, Brown Bear, What Do You See?* He lights up. He beams. He pulls book after book off the shelf, and without words wills us to read them.

Just after he turns two years old, he begins matching pictures in his various books. He finds a photo of a calf in one book and goes running to rummage through the piles in his room. He pulls one out and opens it to the exact right page where there is a painting of a calf. He holds them together for us to see what he's accomplished and smiles. Autistic author and artist Donna Williams writes in her book *Nobody, Nowhere* that matching objects and pictures like this showed her there were definite relationships in the world, relationships in which she might someday be included. And, yes, this is what I see from Ezra. He loves patterns, rhythms, the logic and predictability in the world.

He also loves to hear us count. He jumps on the stepping-stones that travel in a curved line from our front door to the driveway. We wait for him to look up and then we yell out the number: One! He smiles, and jumps to the next one. He looks at us, still smiling. Two! He jumps to the next, looks up. Three! Eleven steps in all. Michael writes the numbers in chalk on the stones, and Ezra's eyes widen with excitement as he sees the connection between our words and the symbols written there.

He finally begins to consistently use sign language for the word "more," and soon thereafter also starts to say "more" with a word that sounds like "ba." On a trip to San Francisco, Michael tickles him on the hotel bed and repeats Ezra's sounds: "A-ha, a-ha." Ezra mimics him—his first real mimic! They go back and forth for a full ten minutes until Ezra finally grows tired of it. Michael laughs and talks animatedly for the rest of the day. These little things can make or break us, just like that.

Defining Normal

I work as a counselor at an alternative high school. They hire me, even though I'm pregnant, and I'm thrilled. This is a job I've wanted for a long time, one where I can meet with teenagers—who are some of my favorite people—and help them navigate through difficulties. Kids attend this school after they've found they can't make it in the regular high school. Most have diagnoses: conduct disorder, oppositional defiance disorder, ADHD, learning disabilities,

two years old

depression, anxiety, OCD, Tourette's syndrome, eating disorders, and one with Asperger's syndrome. They walk through the halls looking like typical teenagers, gossiping, flirting, laughing. They watch me suspiciously as they pass. Every so often I see an autistic kid tromping through the school halls. He's a short, skinny kid with glasses. He smiles at me, just a little, as he walks by.

Ezra is home with Nadine, who has quickly entered my heart. She is a lot like Ezra. She doesn't flinch when I tell her about his speech delays. She is gentle, unimposing, and she and Ezra have taken to each other. I know Ezra likes her soft, almost monotone voice. I feel good knowing he's with her.

During my first week at my new job, Kat, a senior girl with long dark hair, glasses, and a curvaceous figure she intentionally shows off, is sent to see me. She sits on a beat-up chair across from me. She doesn't know me or trust me, as she shouldn't. In general, adults are not easy to trust. She looks down at her lap, picks at her nails. She glances at me, then looks away.

"So, what do you want to know?" she says finally.

I smile. "I don't want to know anything," I say.

She smiles and looks down at her nails.

"I'm serious. You don't have to tell me anything you don't want to."

"They sent me to your office," she says. "I'm sure you want to know why."

"Kat, if you don't want to tell me anything, you don't have to."

She looks up. "You have my file. You can find out anything you want about me."

"That's true."

"I'm sure you already know I'm on meds for depression."

I nod.

She shrugs. "Don't you want to know how that's going?"

"How is that going?" I ask.

"It sucks."

"The medication isn't helping?"

"It is," she says, "but I don't want to have to be on them."

"Why?" I ask.

"Because I don't want to be a freak."

I cock my head. "What makes you think taking meds for depression makes you a freak?"

"Come on. It means I'm crazy."

I laugh. "Not in my mind."

"Well, you're the only one, then."

I look at her a moment, but she's not making eye contact anymore. "Is someone or something making you feel like you're crazy?"

Her head is down. "My dad is a total asshole. He thinks I'm being dramatic."

"That's what he said?"

"A couple times, yeah."

I shake my head. "I'm sorry, Kat. That's not fair to you."

"I just wish I were normal." Tears waver in her eyes. Then she

two years old

starts to cry for real. I sit across from her and wait. I don't pass her tissues, which I always found to be an odd therapy practice, one that suggests we don't want to see their tears. I just wait. After a bit, she stops. She wipes her eyes. "I'm sorry."

"You have nothing to be sorry about," I tell her. "You can be whoever you need to be in here."

She shrugs, uncomfortable. Therapy with teens always has this awkward quality. It's hard not to be embarrassed at this age.

"Kat," I say. "There's no such thing as normal."

She smiles. Tears still cling to her lashes. "I knew you were going to say that eventually. It's what everyone says."

"You don't believe it?"

"You do?" Kat asks, incredulous.

"With all my heart."

She shakes her head. "It's a nice idea in theory, but it doesn't hold true in the real world." She sees me wanting more. "Look around you. All the kids wound up at this school because no one could handle us at the normal school. And then we get here, and even now, at a school where we're all supposed to be freaks, people get teased all the time. There's a popular group, made up of the least-fucked-up kids. I hate my dad, but I'm sure he's just trying to prepare me for real life."

I sit back, sickened by the truth of what she's just said. After a moment, I nod my head.

"You're right," I say. And then I can't help it. I think of Ezra. "This world can be a really shitty place."

SOMETIMES, TO PASS the time during afternoons when I'm not working, friends I made from a moms' group bring their children over to play. I know it's a very bad idea to compare children, and I try hard not to. But it's difficult when these other kids are in front of me, commenting on what they see, asking for things and expressing their discontent in words, while Ezra plays near them, disinterested. I exclaim to the mother of a bilingual boy, "He speaks two languages! That's amazing!" She nods proudly. "We take him camping a lot. Being in nature has really helped his development." I say nothing. What can I say? I know she means nothing by it. I know she has no reason to think saying such a thing might harm me, might start me thinking about all the things I should have done to help Ezra.

Do I blame myself for Ezra's delays? Of course. Of course I do. It is what mothers do. It is even more so what special-needs mothers do. I never took Ezra camping. I never did anything like that. I tried a few activities with him when he was one and a half years old— swimming lessons and music groups—and he cried his way through all of them, overwhelmed by the erratic energy of too many kids, or upset because they played music and it was out of his control.

And then there's the fact that I've also spent a lot of energy trying to carve out time alone, trying to have time away from my child, not because he's unpleasant in any way—quite the opposite— but because I'm selfish like that. I crave time for myself. I've done a lot of things that easily make me feel like I'm a bad mom. I've sat on

two years old

the phone for close to an hour while Ezra entertained himself with a plastic, electronic toy. I've played with him while listening intently for Michael's car to drive up so I can speak with another adult. I've wished for eight o'clock to come so I can just put him to sleep. I've let him flip through books on the floor while I read my own, each of us doing our own thing.

My friend Terri, who eventually became an ex-friend, said once, "Well, do you talk to Ezra enough?" She said, "Maybe he's just reacting to your stress." She said, "You're always assuming he's going to act a certain way. You need to lay off him." She said, "I don't believe in things like autism. Parents cause their children to behave certain ways." Just like when Denis Leary said there's no such thing as autism, only inattentive moms, thinking he was being funny. With each comment, I sink deeper. I lose my grip on anything I believed before, what I thought I knew, or who I thought I was as a parent.

I go back further to Ezra's birth, starting finally this search for reasons. Starting down this now well-worn path I must travel—that all mothers typically travel when they have a special-needs child. His head was posterior, and so I was in early labor for three days, in immense pain. I wound up choosing an epidural and Pitocin, drugs to which I never wanted to expose my baby. I was so exhausted that I pushed for almost four hours. He sat in the birth canal, distressed, and came out with green meconium, his first bowel movement, so they suppressed his breathing for a few minutes while they made sure his lungs were clear. Is this where it began? Did he not receive enough oxygen to his brain? I think of that army of pediatricians who marched into the delivery room. They had been hovering, waiting for their grand entrance. I hated them then for scooping up my baby, pulling him off my chest, where he was animal warm, to perform their cruel, clinical work. But, of course, it's unlikely I'd be able to prove that this was the cause, and even if I could, what would I do? Sue? Nothing can change what is.

After Ezra's birth the doctors forgot to give me a catheter, and I couldn't urinate on my own for almost three weeks. I suffered through a urinary tract infection and had to take antibiotics, leading to thrush for both Ezra and me. After trying every natural solution, to no effect, I finally gave him Diflucan at six weeks old. So, here he was, poisoned with thrush, with yeast, which so many naturopaths blame for all sorts of diseases, including autism. Was it this?

I also let him be vaccinated. My God, I let him be vaccinated! It's true that we didn't receive the shots until he was older than most babies on the immunization schedule, and I only let him have some—not all—of the vaccines. It's true that he didn't get the MMR. He never regressed. He didn't seem to have any ill effects from the vaccines. Still, I allowed for Ezra this item that scientists and conspiracy theorists alike have argued back and forth, have gone back to again and again, regardless of scientific studies proving otherwise, as a possible cause of autism.

two years old

There is strong precedent for an autistic child's mother's guilt. Only a little over half a century ago, child psychologist Bruno Bettelheim claimed that the cause of autism was a mother's unconscious wish that her child didn't exist. Bettelheim called them refrigerator mothers. Children were institutionalized, and the mothers were treated for supposedly not wanting their children. It's outrageous to think of today, but that was the overarching theory at the time about autism. I think how easy it is to feel guilty and responsible for who my child is, for the ways he isn't typical.

Imagine those mothers, both blamed by the medical community and surely internalizing their own worries. Obviously they had it much worse, but amazing how that blame still exists subtly from people like that "friend" who doesn't believe autism is real, from the pressure to do something, quickly, now, before it's too late. I should have done something then. I should be doing something now. I should always, always be doing something. Yet if I do something, Ezra winds up stressed and unhappy. If I do nothing, I fear I'm not helping him. So I do the bare minimum, and I worry it's the wrong thing and not enough and I keep worrying more.

I cannot keep burdening Michael with these worries. Ezra is his son, too, and I don't want to frighten him. Twice he's asked me, "Should I be worrying?" *No!* I say. Because I can't have Michael overly concerned. If he worries with me, who will pull me back? Who will keep us from falling more deeply into this endless fear?

Ezra has some words now. He says the word "more," and he

touches my belly and says "baby," and he can say "ball" and "car" and "please" and "book." He learns more sign language from his video. He also can verbally put a few words together, at our urging: "Read book." When he reaches for my hand to try to pull me somewhere, I teach him to say, "Come, Mama." It sounds like "Um, Ama" when he says it. Dave, the speech therapist, is mightily impressed. He tells me, "This guy is going to be a talker, I'm sure of it." I ask him to say it again, to tell me why he says that. I want someone to tell me my son will be okay.

I buy a few books on autism. Just a few for now. In the future, I will have a four-foot shelf solely for books about autism and therapies and autism memoirs. For now, I order just a few. Their titles, *Your Quirky Child*, *The Out-of-Sync Child*, and *The Child with Special Needs*, speak so much to the fact that I'm not sure yet what to look for. Also, there is a notable lack of the word "autism" in the names. I am most moved by Stanley Greenspan's book, which describes Floortime, something I realize I already do with Ezra. It is the first time, actually, I feel some sort of nod from the outside world: *Yes, you are doing the right thing for your child.*

Floortime engages the child by allowing him to lead. So, for instance, if Ezra pushes a car along the floor, as he often does, I take another car and crash it into his. Always, Ezra laughs, and often it prompts him to say "more."

He has always found toys crashing and falling and smashing to be funny. The first time he laughed really hard about something other than one of us tickling him or trying to make him laugh was when he was nine months old. We were at the beginning of a trailhead with friends, and a young boy there was whacking at bushes with a stick. Ezra thought this was the funniest thing he had ever seen. So, anyway, I thought I was just serving myself, wanting to hear Ezra's laugh, wanting us to laugh together, when I crashed his car. But here I learn I'm doing Floortime, a well-respected therapy.

Still, sometimes I see the worry starting in Michael. Worry. It reclines on the couch, its sticky arm slung over autism's shoulders. It bounces its knee, taps its foot, drums its fingers, always moving, always noisy and disruptive. It won't shut up. It won't settle down. It twitters through the house, jumping and skipping, until finally Michael can no longer ignore it. Michael holds a picture of a cat in front of Ezra and says, "What is this, Ezra? Tell me what this is." Ezra doesn't respond, as usual, and the muscle in Michael's jaw twitches, worry working its way under his skin.

WE GO TO the birthday parties of kids from the moms' group. At one, a child sits coloring a picture, and Ezra toddles over and takes a crayon.

"Ee ee ee!" the little girl yells, so I take the crayon from Ezra and hand it back to the girl.

Then Ezra walks right into the middle of a game a group of kids are playing.

"Hey!" they yell. I steer him away.

Then he reaches for an ornament hanging from the Christmas tree they still have up.

"I'm sorry," I tell him. "You have to put that back." I take it from his hands and hang it back up myself. He walks on, looking for something he's allowed to do. I stay behind him, my eyes on everything he does.

The other parents mingle. They drink their wine and chat, letting their children play. I wish I could do the same. After a while they sing the birthday song, and I tense up, afraid Ezra will cry hearing this song he knows sung out of tune, or just not quite the way he wants. He doesn't cry, but he does pull me outside, away from the singing and festivities, and where he can rub his hands on the mud in a little puddle near the side of the house. I can see the party through the sliding glass door, and I can't help but feel frustrated and alone. The childish part of me wishes someone would see us out here, would keep us company, but I'm aware that's unfair. Why should anyone else miss out on the fun if they don't have to? I have to. That's the simple truth. But it's also the reason I stop going to these parties. I stop reaching out to these friends, these parents who can't begin to understand my experience as a mother, even if they wanted to, which I doubt most of them do.

My friends also tire of me. I ask them too many questions— *Did you see the way Ezra did that? Do you think he's okay? Is that*

two years old

something most two-year-olds do? Terri lets me know that our child therapist friend told her in confidence that my concern about Ezra was getting old. She told me this perhaps as a way to let me know herself that my concerns were boring her. My friends are tired of hearing me run over the same things again and again. They're tired of watching me grow elated over some small new development and then defeated as something else falls back or doesn't progress enough. I'm hormonal and anxious. I'm no longer counseling at the school, which took my mind off my fears about Ezra at least a little. I'm about to give birth to a baby, a baby I'm second-guessing, which makes me feel even worse. I stop talking about the worry, because I know it's not welcome and because, honestly, I'm sick of it, too, but all I feel as a result of not talking about it is alone.

Perhaps this is why when Michael sees a job on the East Coast, in a Massachusetts town where we could live in my late grandparents' condominium for free, where we'd be just a few hours' drive from family and friends we miss, I encourage him to apply. It's something we've considered since Ezra's birth. While we both spent most of our single lives in bars and at parties, moving from one house share to another, from one girlfriend or boyfriend to another, once we became a family and all of that dropped away, we felt ungrounded. We realized we didn't come from here. We wanted grandparents for our kids. We wanted aunts and uncles and all the cousins who live back East.

The company calls him a few days later, and by the following week, we're faced with the decision to move. We stand together, holding hands, my big belly between us. We smile nervously. Should we do it? We take out paper and pen and make a list of pros and cons. We glance at each other. Should we do it? There's no question that the idea of this move, the hugeness of it, feels exciting. There's no question that we're both thinking—but not saying—that the move holds the promise of change, not just in terms of where we live, but possibly in terms of our concerns about Ezra. It's not a rational thought. Obviously, moving to the other side of the country will not transform Ezra into a typically developing child. It won't make the worry or the autism go away. Surely they will come with us, settling with us into our new home. Surely neither will stay here without us, even though we foolishly hope they will.

But we decide to go, and we start to make plans. Meanwhile, I have to have this baby, and I do, that night, actually, while Ezra is sleeping. We head to the hospital, letting Nadine know as we leave. We go up the elevator to the maternity ward, our minds on the move. I don't even feel the contractions anymore, actually. I'm convinced it's false labor and that once they check me they will send me back home.

But I go to pee, and there is my mucous plug. The doctor on call snaps on a glove and reaches inside me, and it turns out I'm seven centimeters dilated, with a bulging bag of waters. I'm about to go into transition. Michael and I laugh and chat animatedly. This is so different from our last experience. We can hardly believe

two years old

it. The contractions grow difficult. I animal-moan through them. The nurses are there, and Michael, whom I push away and pull toward me, his shirt twisted inside my fist. And then a contraction comes that I can't yell over, and my water breaks. Suddenly, I'm lying back and pushing, and out comes Griffin, just like that.

I hold his tiny red body, and Michael and I kiss his little eyes and nose. He has a full head of hair, just like Ezra did, but Griffin's is brown, not blond. Like Ezra, he nurses immediately and easily. We refuse everything the hospital recommends for Griffin, just like we did for Ezra: no shots, no circumcision, no eye goop, no nothing. An angry pediatrician named Dr. Julie, who doesn't like when parents think they know what's best, comes to the room for a visit. She says to us, "Your baby could die if you don't do these things." Then we sign a release that states we are leaving against medical advice, and we go home.

In the morning, Michael brings Ezra upstairs. Ezra had no idea we were even gone, that this stupendous thing happened in the night. He comes onto the bed, and I show him his new baby brother, who is swaddled tight. I don't know how this will go, if Ezra will benefit from this tiny new person who is about to enter his life. Ezra glances at the baby, and then he sees a book on the floor. He goes to pick it up.

"Ezra," I say. "Come here, come see the baby. Do you see the baby?"

Ezra ignores me.

"Look," I say. I move near him, where he stares intently at a page in the book. "Do you see the baby?"

He looks at Griffin finally, just for a beat. "Baby," he says, appeasing me. Then he's back to the book.

Six weeks later, we board a plane to Massachusetts.

Spring in Massachusetts

FOUR YEARS OLD

Adaptive Behavior

Our first week in the Berkshires, which is on the westernmost edge of Massachusetts, we stay in a hotel. Nadine will join us in a couple weeks, once we have moved into the condo. Michael and I have gone through difficulty before, when I had an early miscarriage before my pregnancy with Ezra. That was a rough time. I felt hopeless. I worried there was something wrong with my body, with me. I understood that I could be on the losing end of statistics, which had never happened to me before. I had always been lucky. I had always been charmed. Michael had to find a way to help me through, to be there for me, to encourage me and keep me optimistic. He was good at that, and eventually I was pregnant again. But this is different. This is far beyond anything we know how to do. We're in way over our heads. We didn't think this through. We were already struggling with concerns about Ezra. We were already not at our best. But now we have piled on a move, and not just to another house. We moved to another world, far away from everything we know. Michael has to start a new job. We don't know where we are. We don't know where anything is. We don't know who we are here. We don't yet have a home. We have a brand-new baby and a child whom we don't understand. What have we done? In this tiny, boxed-in room where the four of us have to live until we can move into the condo, we look at each other briefly, then look away. We can't admit this terrible mistake.

Outside, snow pads the ground. Black, craggy trees stand against the cold white sky floating down in prism flakes to the lake below. As a child, I spent a lot of time in this town. I visited my grandparents during the summer months. I went with them to the country club, where they taught me to play golf. We drove along the rural roads until we came to a natural spring fountain. We pulled empty glass bottles from the trunk and filled them with the icy water. In winter, my parents, sister, and I came up from New Jersey and learned to ski. And then, after my parents' divorce, my mother drove up here with my sister and me during winter breaks from school. We knew the names of the ski lift operators. We knew where the Price Chopper was, and the natural-food store, and the antique shops where you could buy penny candy from jars. We knew the woman who owned the store, which was full of hand-knit sweaters and hats. We knew the galleries and the man who scooped

four years old

ice cream at the creamery. In the midst of a turbulent adolescence, during a time of loss and yearning and desperation, I felt safe here. I thought back then that this would be the perfect place to live when I grew up.

Now, Ezra stands at the window, watching the wet spring snow falling flatly to the ground. He is my child, my love, but I don't know what it is he's thinking about, what he needs from me at any moment. I hold Griffin in my arms. Back in my adolescence, did I imagine what my life would be? Not really. But then, none of us can know what our lives will bring.

We drive to see the condominium. My mother and her soon-to-be-husband, Charlie, arrived yesterday to help empty it. The home is still packed full with my grandparents' things—cracked dishes and old mail and books and framed photos and clothes. They have so much stuff. Mountains of boxes in storage, paintings, furniture, souvenirs from travels, broken items they meant to have fixed. Strange to see it now, all the things we concern ourselves with, but then in the end we just die and leave it for someone else to throw out. My mother starts to work, filling boxes and Dumpsters, determining what to save and store. Charlie tries to keep the atmosphere light, exclaiming over my grandfather's war medals, old medical documents. I know this is hard for my mother. My grandmother died just recently. My grandfather died nearly a decade before. She was close with her parents in a way I'm not close with her. Actually, I was also close with her parents in a way I am not close with her.

At one point, before she leaves town and Michael and I move in, she and I have a fight. It's inevitable. She wants me to be more appreciative of the work she's doing to clean out the condo. I want her to just do it for me, without needing anything back.

A memory: my mother and sister and me in a parking lot. I'm ten years old. My mother grasps at our hands, and I pull my hand away. It's instinct, what I always do. I'm always the one pulling away. I can't help it. That grasping, the need that's always there, all the ways she needed me to provide something for her, something I desperately didn't want to have to give away. But my sister accepts her hand. She accepts so much when it comes to Mom. She's better at that than I am. Or maybe she really doesn't mind. The two of them take off, skipping toward the car. My mother barely looks back at me. They are off, my mother screeching and giggling like a child, my sister silent and smiling, always compliant. I hate them. Much more than that, I love them. I stand alone on the sidewalk, watching, always watching.

Here we are, twenty-five years later. My mother is sad about her parents. I'm lost and confused about my life. We are exactly the same people we were all those years ago. She needs me to care for her needs. I need her to put my needs before hers, especially right now, when things are so frightening. So we argue, and then we each lean on the person who will understand us, who will see the world the way we each see it. I turn to Michael; she turns to Charlie. And then we part ways.

four years old

MICHAEL AND I sit in the car and drive. We drive and drive, trying to gain a sense of where we are. We go to a town I remember from my past, a town where I once met a boy I thought I loved, where I spent the evening wishing he were still mine. We stop at a health-food market, put Ezra and Griffin in his car seat into a cart. We find some familiar items—Ezra's cookies and the diapers I like. Ezra reaches for a wooden spatula for sale, and Michael takes it down and starts a game with it. Ezra giggles. This is when a woman with black frizzy hair approaches us.

"Oh!" she exclaims, seeing tiny Griffin, who is asleep. "Is this your baby brother?" she asks Ezra, who ignores her, still laughing with Michael. "Is it?" she asks again. "Do you like your little brother?"

I sense immediately what is about to come, can feel its sharp fingers poking before it starts. This is an irony of having a child with autism: While autistic people are notoriously, and often misperceived as being, clueless about other people, the parents of autistic children develop sharp radar. We are too aware of others' thoughts, too conscious of people's determinations.

She finds me at the checkout line. "Can I talk to you a moment?" she asks. I try to look preoccupied, to be so involved with placing the groceries onto the belt that I don't have a moment for anything else. But it's amazing how many supposedly normal people don't pay attention to social cues. I wish I had said, "Nope. Too busy." But I stupidly, nervously, let her take me aside. My heart sits in my throat. I know exactly what's coming.

"Have you ever heard of autism?" she asks.

I wish I had said, "Ever heard of condescension?" But instead, I say, "Of course."

She says, "We have a great program just south of here, a program that can help."

I know the program of which she speaks. I saw it amid one of my many research marathons, trying to determine what I should be doing for Ezra. I know that the program's headquarters are based in Sheffield, which is just south of here, like she says. The basic philosophy of the program she refers to is that we must "love the child," be fun and kind, and laugh with them to bring them back from autism. I know she thinks she means well. I know she believes I need her, that so many people need her. We all have our ways of feeling worthwhile in the world. But while she's concerning herself with her heroics, while she thinks she's doing good, I am shrinking. I wish I could just say this. I wish I could just say, "Do you have any idea what this is like, to have a stranger stop me in a store and tell me my son is not okay?"

I wish I could say, "Have you ever considered that saying this might not be noble to some of us? That most parents already deeply love their autistic children, already laugh and have fun with them, and have spent a lot of time and energy and money to do our best for them on our own terms? Have you ever considered that most parents know their children better than you or your cult organization ever could?"

I wish I could say, "Actually, I have some advice for that hair of yours. Use oil. Oh, you don't like having a stranger making note of your atypical hair in a store, thinking she should tell you how to take care of it?"

I wish I could say, "Do you have a child who's autistic? No? Then shut the fuck up and mind your own business, you frizzy-haired bitch." But I say, "Thank you," and spend the rest of the day—the rest of my life, probably—wishing I hadn't.

MICHAEL GOES OFF to his new job each day, and I try to settle us into the condo. I put the boys into the car and drive, trying to find what we need. What we need is such a humungous concept. So impossible to fill, it seems. So I stick to the tangible essentials. I discover a Target and buy shower curtains and paper towels. I find a store that carries Ezra's cheese puffs and cookies. Since the move, he won't eat pizza, the one item he ate that seemed like food. I try not to fret about this, to let it pull me down. Surely, he will eat pizza again.

My friend from college visits with her two girls. One is a few months younger than Ezra, the other a few months older than Griffin. I adore my friend Kristin. She is almost always magically happy. Her smile is constant and genuine. She is probably the sweetest person I've ever known. She lived in Portland for a year before heading back East and marrying David, her college sweetheart. They struggled with infertility, made difficult decisions about it, but now have these two beautiful girls.

Ezra plays with his toys, ignoring everyone, except for once coming over to smile at the baby and touch her soft hair. The older girl talks on the phone with her father and says, "Mommy says I can watch a movie later. What movie do I get to watch, Daddy?" and I try not to feel distraught. I try not to compare.

My friend says, "I'm so glad you guys are here. We're so excited to be able to see you now!" She's so positive. She's always been like this. It's something I love about her. But right now, I can't feel anything beyond my fears and regrets. Everything is far in the distance, on the other side of a blurry lens. Everything feels like what I have to move through until something feels better.

And also, there's something I'm not telling you. Something I've told no one. Something I'm thinking about often because it feels better than thinking about anything else right now. I'm in contact with an old flame, who lives just two hours from where we are now, a boy I fell in love with years ago, before Michael, before I became a mother, responsible, weighted. Before I became a person whose life felt suddenly heavy with too many things she didn't understand.

It's inevitable, isn't it, that I turn to that old habit again now, where I escape into the possibility of a new man? Also, though, it makes no sense. It's the worst thing I could do. I have a new baby, a son who needs my very best. I have a husband who is slipping, falling into *his* old habit of going mute, depressed, away from me. If I were a better person, if I were a stronger person, perhaps I would do something different. I want to be that person. I want to

four years old

be what everyone needs me to be. But I'm not. And so this is where I go. I turn my focus outward. I try to lose myself in the fantasy of another life. And in my defense, I don't really go anywhere. I just meet Frank for lunch in West Stockbridge.

Seven years earlier, before I met Michael, I came to West Stockbridge to interview for a teaching position at an alternative preparatory high school. During that visit, I took a field trip in a van full of teenage students—who perhaps, I imagined at the time, were not unlike my own unborn children would be—to a small gallery where the kids' art was on display. I remember buying a ring from the gallery, a wide band of sterling silver. To meet Frank here now feels right. It feels weighted with impressions from the past, from a time when I wasn't married, when I didn't have a special-needs child, when my body wasn't still recovering from birth just two months earlier.

Originally, I met Frank when I was twenty-six years old, at an artists' retreat in Vermont. He was married, not totally unhappily, but something about our connection threw him. He liked my perspective. I liked how he talked about his painting, and how he looked evenly out into the world. He was a total babe. But he was *married*. I was a mess when it came to relationships, but I wasn't an idiot. I had lost enough in love to know it made no sense to throw myself at a man who was already taken. Still, he pursued me, and though we never did more than have a few drunken kisses, we had built a real friendship on the phone and via email ever since.

Now Frank and I meet here in this halfway place, a place reminiscent of how our lives could have been had he taken the chance and left his wife. Also, however, it's a place I walk through now as a married woman holding my newborn, my breasts not heaving with passion, just heavy with milk letdown for Griffin.

We hug awkwardly, the baby between us, and find a spot on the grass for a picnic. I uncork a bottle of wine and we drink. Not the whole bottle, mind you, but a few cups. We discuss his marriage and my trip east, all while I grow tipsy. Griffin sleeps briefly and then nurses, growing tipsy too, I imagine, from the sweet wine in my milk.

Frank hands me a CD he made for our meeting, and we take a drive through the Berkshire landscape and listen. He includes songs with titles such as "Still in Love" and "Two-Headed Boy," heartbreaking songs with lyrics that I only really hear later, when it's just me and Griffin in the car, no longer tipsy but still heady with thoughts of the day. Each song makes me want to turn around, all the way around, back to when we were twenty-six and unencumbered, to find him again.

At home, I find Ezra playing with Nadine. More accurately, he plays with a toy and Nadine watches him. He sticks a letter into the slot and presses the button, and it plays a recording about the letter. He repeats his favorite again and again, in hysterics. "V-v-v-vibrating!" he yells. He looks up at me, his eyes bright and alive. He wants me to laugh with him, to see how impossibly funny this is. *V-v-v-vibrating! Is there anything more wonderful?* In the middle of all the craziness, Ezra is the only one who seems to be keeping it together. He has his things. His people. He's doing just fine.

The baby, who has recently begun to notice more of the world around him, sees his brother and coos, his arms waving. He's doing fine, too.

Later, when Michael comes home from work and Ezra is in his bath, Michael steps around the living room, picking up toys. "For God's sake!" he yells when he steps down on a Lego. In the Portland house, we had a separate playroom. Here, we've smashed our lives together with the kids'. We left a lot of toys in storage boxes, but still, the walls press in on us. There is not a spot of floor that doesn't seem littered with toys. I'm okay with it, but I can tell it's making Michael insane. He grew up with seven brothers and sisters. He never had his own space, or time for himself. He told me many times early in our relationship that he needs privacy, and he needs it often. But I'm still annoyed that he can't be positive right now, that when everything is unraveling, he just lets it unravel. I'm annoyed that he keeps moving away from me when I need him to stay.

"Can you at least try to be happy?" I say.

"No," he says. "I can't. I'm living in a shoebox in a place I don't like."

He glares at me. I know he blames me. It always comes down to this for us. I assume we're making decisions together, but then it seems I'm always the one responsible for them.

"I didn't put a gun to your head," I say, although the thought of a gun to his head right now is mighty pleasing.

"You told me this condominium was big enough for all of us. You told me I'd want to live in this godforsaken town."

I want to say, *Stay strong. Don't go away. I need you.* But I'm too angry, too goddamn angry and lonely. So I walk into the other room.

A few days later, I find Ezra pressing buttons on a toy. There is something all over his shirt, and a weird smell. I move closer. What the hell?

"Ezra!" I yell. "No!" I lay the baby on the ground near the bathroom and pick up Ezra. The baby cries. Ezra also starts to cry. I turn on the water in the bathtub, which drowns their screaming, and I yank Ezra's poop-smeared shirt over his head. His hands are covered with poop. It's on his back above his diaper. I tear off the diaper. "Stay still," I tell Ezra as calmly as I can. "Don't touch anything. Don't touch!" I yell as he goes to hold my arm. I drop him in the bath, gather washcloths, and start scrubbing. Ezra hates to be scrubbed. Good. Maybe he won't do it again.

Nadine comes running in. She is off-duty today. "What happened?"

"Nothing," I say. I'm too distraught to tell her, too frightened. I don't want to see her look of horror. I don't want her to decide she can't do this job. She catches my tight energy and leaves us alone.

Once he's clean and the waste has gone down the drain, I

four years old

fill the bath and let Ezra sit in it for a while. I pick up Griffin, who stopped crying after a while, realizing he wasn't going to be attended to, and I sit on the closed toilet lid and nurse him. Only in the calm can I consider more intently what's just happened: Ezra was playing with his own feces. I've heard of mothers who find their babies in their crib after naps, rubbing their own poop on the walls, the sheets, and the crib rails. I also remember a commonly told story in college about a sophomore who smeared his shit after taking acid.

What is wrong with my child?

Ezra laughs now, dipping toy fish in and out of the water. "Red fish!" he says. "Orange fish!" He can't pronounce his *d*'s, *r*'s, or *f*'s, but as long as there's a context, I understand him.

"Ezra," I say.

He doesn't look at me.

"You don't ever touch poopy with your hands. Do you hear me?"

Nothing.

"Ezra."

"Blue fish!"

I give up. I have to hope he won't do it again. Later, a lot of parents tell me stories of their neurotypical kids or friends with neurotypical kids who do the same thing, so I throw it onto my mental list of Ezra's behaviors that may or may not stem from autism.

The following week, driving with Griffin asleep in his seat, I have a car accident. It isn't a normal accident. I'm at a stoplight and a semi truck next to me moves forward when the light turns green, squeezing the frame of my car against the curb.

I beep the horn. "Stop!" I yell.

There is an explosion, and the rear window shatters into millions of pieces.

Griffin starts screaming. I join him. The truck releases us and I drive to the side of the street, yelling, "My baby! I have a baby!"

The semi pulls behind me. I jump out of the car, my heart rocketing through my chest, and pull Griffin out. I unbuckle him and hold him close, pressing my face into his soft hair while he cries. He is unharmed. The shattered glass fell just around the window, and thankfully, none came near the baby. I take deep breaths, trying to calm myself. The truck driver checks in on us and gives me his information, and I call Michael with the news. I've never had a car accident in my life and I have no clue how to proceed, so he takes over. He calls the insurance company and has a rental car sent to me. Eventually the car is fixed, but it's never the same again. The fact of the accident stays with me, feeds the fear inside me that this move was all wrong and foreshadows a different sort of tragedy. Any time the car has a mechanical problem, I remember that impact, the squeezing, the terror that shot through me during the accident when the window exploded and Griffin screamed. I'm petrified that my family won't be released— but from what, exactly, I don't yet know.

. . .

four years old

First Steps

I need to find therapists for Ezra again. Of all the things we left in Portland, our speech therapist, Patti, was probably the most regrettable. When I whined to her that we'd never find anyone as wonderful, as understanding, as sensitive to who Ezra was, she said, "Oh, I'm sure you'll find someone great." But I knew better.

I look up the number for Early Intervention, call First Steps in Massachusetts, and dial, my stomach heavy with dread. I hated Early Intervention in Oregon, but I don't know where else to begin. It might be different here in Massachusetts. They might have better funding, which would mean better services. And it's free. Ezra turns three in just a few months, but they tell me we can start as soon as possible. When he turns three, he'll have to go to preschool to be helped. This policy is the same as Oregon's. It's the same all over the country. This would be fine, I suppose, if I felt Ezra were anywhere near ready to go to school. But he's not. He's developmentally behind. He barely speaks, and when he does his articulation is dreadful. He communicates differently than other children. He has no social skills. Before I knew about Early Intervention's rules, I had decided I would not let him go to school before he turned four. Now I feel pressured, and I don't like it one bit. I don't like that we're supposed to hand over our children so young. I don't like that we're expected to parade our developmentally different children in front of other people and children, who will do what they do. I don't like that this is expected, that it's assumed we're at a loss on our own, that we're supposed to need them and their evaluating eyes and behavioral approaches and determinations about who our children need to be.

None of it feels right to me. When we worked with Patty, we had an out, but in this tiny section of the United States I can't seem to locate any private practitioners. Everyone works for a hospital or some kind of organization. Everyone has to fill out forms and reach outcome standards, as if children are simply cogs in a machine that will result in funding for the agency. All my instincts say no, and if I've learned anything from our previous efforts at receiving therapy, it's to trust my instincts.

This is, of course, my own fault—Michael's and mine—for moving here, away from a therapist we felt good about. For feeling desperate enough in our pain to make a dumb decision that we couldn't just take back. But what's done is done. It makes no sense to wade around in regret. While Ezra is still two, we accept that he will have to receive services through First Steps. This also means, of course, we will have to have another evaluation.

Three evaluators walk through my door once more. Three evaluators again eye Ezra. One carries a tote of toys, just like before. Another carries a ream of papers to scan and sign. This time, I tell them right off the bat. I say, "I don't want this evaluation. I just want people who will get down on the floor with my son, who will be willing to follow him into his world to help him learn. If at any point he starts to be upset, this evaluation will be over."

They nod and smile. They try their best to look like they take me seriously. They aren't used to parents' having opinions. I'm quite sure at least one of them makes a mental note: high-needs parent, in denial about what her child needs. You see, I still don't quite get it. They will always value their evaluations over my child. They will never stop believing that my son should be someone else to be okay in the world. They will pose it differently, of course. They'll think, *This boy needs to be changed if he's ever going to be happy.* They'll think, *This mother is doing her child a disservice by thinking he's okay as he is.* We will never, ever find that place in the middle, where my son can be both supported and helped in the areas he is challenged in and where he can also feel good about who he is. For reasons I don't understand, this will never be possible in the minds of so many of the evaluators we meet.

So, here we go again.

Here is Ezra: He wants to play. He just wants to play. But they keep putting new things before him on a little tray. There's a particular way he has to play with them, or else he will fail. They give him puzzles he's done a million times before, puzzles he can do blindfolded, but because he's upset that they took away the other toy, the one he wanted, the one he felt like playing with, he doesn't do the puzzle, and he fails. They show him another toy and tell him something. To him, it sounds like gibberish. It sounds like pointless adult rambling, about which he doesn't care. He ignores them, reaches for the toy. *No, no,* they say, and they hide the toy beneath a cloth. Ezra begins to whimper. He reaches for the cloth, and they snatch up the toy and hide it somewhere else. Ezra begins to cry, giving up, and they mark it on their tidy form. He fails.

But failing leads to the speech therapist he needs, which is the whole point. Her name is Julie. She comes once a week and brings toys Ezra likes, and she does the frustrating-the-child thing with him until he says what she wants him to say. We also are assigned a behavioral psychologist every other week, who does pretty much the same thing the speech therapist does, except she also gives us tips on how to teach him to wait and share, things most other almost-three-year-olds are learning as well.

We don't meet anyone who seems to know anything about why he isn't eating. I know all about sensory issues by now. I've read everything I can find about why a child might eat only two things—cheese puffs and cookies—neither which is nutritious, and yet nothing seems to fit for Ezra. The assumed reason would be that he has issues with texture, but this isn't the case. Although he doesn't eat more than these two things, at one point he ate items that each had entirely different textures. And he will put a variety of textured items in his mouth that aren't food. He was a champion breastfeeder, stopping just recently, right before Griffin was born. He mouthed things, like most babies, and then stopped when most toddlers do, and only more recently started with the pica. It's all so confusing.

In my quest to help him, I suck it up for one more evaluation, this time from an occupational therapist at the local hospital. I explain to her my concerns. Her name is . . . I don't remember her name. There are simply too many of them. And besides, soon she'll be gone on maternity leave, and they'll assign us someone new whom Ezra doesn't like, and so we'll have to move on, putting this therapy experience behind us with all the rest. No offense to her, because is was nice enough and I know she tries her best, but she would't have made a difference for Ezra anyway. For now, hope alive, she gives me a sensory profile to fill out, the same one I've been given twice before, the same one that doesn't address my son's particular issue, because, like most people, he doesn't fit into a mold. Most people I meet seem to know this already, that humans are messy, unpredictable creatures, and that each one is different from the next. But the world of experts is still lagging on this matter, at least when it comes to examining special needs, and especially when it comes to *children* with special needs. No matter. I fill out the form while Ezra jumps into a tub of balls. I can't imagine how this is going to help his eating, but at least he's having fun.

MEMORIAL DAY WEEKEND, we give Nadine the long weekend off and drive three hours to stay with Michael's sister. Most of Michael's family will be there, with a lot of nieces and nephews. We're excited. This is what we moved here for, to be closer to family we love, so Ezra and Griffin can know their many cousins, aunts, and uncles. When Michael and I were dating, one of the reasons I knew I wanted to marry him was for his family. They seemed so normal. So different from my own crazy family, from the isolation I felt from them. I had always craved a family like this—warm and loud and kind. So we drive past the changing landscape of oaks and pine, past farmland and billboards, tightly packed houses and buildings puffing out black smoke, and the brick box apartment buildings that house the millions of people who live in the tri-state area.

On our first day, Ezra hides in the basement, away from the other children's high energy. He watches his Elmo video again and again. When one of the cousins goes down to play, he cries, wanting to be alone. Eventually, Michael and I tire of being stuck down there, so we come upstairs. When I check on him, he has poop on his hands and he's busy grinding it into my sister-in-law's carpet with his foot. Horrified, mortified, I scoop him up.

"I'm so sorry," I tell my sister-in-law.

"Come on," she says. "Kids do things. They mess things up. Don't worry."

"I think I got it all out of the carpet." I look at the cup of coffee in my hands. If I say much more, I'll start crying, and if I start crying I fear I won't be able to stop. That can't happen here, not now, not with my pleasant, normal in-laws.

My sister-in-law tells me about how one of her friend's children—a neurotypical child—used to do the same thing, and how her friend felt the same way: horrified, helpless, unable to figure out how to make it stop. She promised me that when that child potty-trained, it was over.

Upstairs, we hear the water splashing where Michael is bathing the feces off Ezra. "It's a banner day for Ezra," my sister-in-law says. "He played with his poop, and now he gets to take a bath." We laugh. She's so good at making things light like this, so good at empathizing, at making me feel like my little family isn't as freaky as I sometimes feel it is.

But the next day is a repeat of the last, including the ground poop. We planned to stay the whole weekend, but after just one night we decide to drive back. Some situations just feel too hard, like too much work. It won't always be like this. Or will it? I guess I don't know yet. This kind of thinking has always saved me: *Things feel impossible now, but nothing is static. There will always be change. Someday, Ezra won't play with his poop. I have to believe that. It sustains me.*

Although she did everything she could to make us comfortable, there's no missing the concern in Michael's sister's face as we tell her we're going to go. I know his family well enough to be sure that as soon as we leave, the phone calls will begin—not to us, no, but to the other sisters. Phone calls about how something is terribly wrong with Ezra, how sorry they all feel for our fate. Even with our extended family, we will feel outside of the circle, unable to experience what they can. It's no one's fault, just the truth. We have only one another.

NOW THAT EZRA is no longer breastfeeding, I worry about his nutrition. I need to find a way to supplement his nearly nonexistent diet. Also, he's often constipated, sometimes so much so that we have to use a glycerin suppository, which leads to a lot of screaming. So I go online to look for a naturopath, and this is where I come across the world of DAN! doctors. DAN! stands for Defeat Autism Now, with an exclamation point! I know they have the best intentions, that they truly believe they are helping autistic children and their families. I know there is sound practice, based on some semblance of sound research. But also, a lot of DAN! doctors are caught up in the idea that we can pound autism out of kids' systems. That if we just insert the right combination of *antioxidants . . . supplements . . . chelating agents . . . B_{12} . . . methylators . . . probiotics . . . antivirals . . . enzymes* (they will try absolutely *anything*), then your child could be normal (exclamation point!). They are fully convinced, as anyone is who lives and breathes a certain theory, that they are right. Even when there is evidence to counteract their beliefs, they consider it to be only a hiccup, an outlier of everything else that points to their truth.

There are millions of DAN! parents who also believe this theory, regardless of science and FDA approvals. That's what happens when there are no clear answers, when we are dealing with a condition that we know so little about, and when parents feel helpless to aid their children. Like what happened in the nineteenth century, when no one knew why people were getting consumption, and the

four years old

cure was believed to be purging and bloodletting and heliotherapy. People believed evil spirits and vapors and unnamable corruptions in the body caused the symptoms. Until finally a scientist discovered the bacteria that we now know cause tuberculosis.

But I'm getting ahead of myself once again, because when I first discover the world of DAN! doctors, I don't feel this way about them at all. I feel hopeful. I feel excited. I feel the same way I still can to this day when someone tells me that some potion or treatment or mixture led to a child with no issues. I'm cynical, sure. I'm always cynical, as you might have already guessed. But do I want my son to eat food? Yes, indeed I do. Do I want him to catch up in his speech and learn how to have a conversation? Absolutely. Will I try something that has done these things for others? Of course I will.

So I find one of these doctors in a nearby town. His name is Dr. Kevin Destroyer. It isn't really. I won't use his real name. But his last name is as scary as the one I've created here. He has his MD, as opposed to an ND, which is notable only because most DAN! doctors are naturopaths. While I'm a fan of naturopaths and their complement to traditional medicine, there is a false sense of validity that comes along with the idea of a medical doctor. You think MDs will be more conservative, less willing to try dangerous, unsubstantiated treatments, which can often come along with the world of DAN!

The DAN! medical doctor talks with me while Ezra plays. He barely looks at Ezra, except to awkwardly tell him not to come back behind his desk. Dr. Destroyer tells me about all the exciting research. He has trouble looking me in the eye. Truth be told, I think Dr. Destroyer might be somewhere on the spectrum. He says a few things that concern me:

"It's great that he's playing with toys and interacting with his environment. Let's get in there quickly before he loses any of those skills."

"All kids on the autistic spectrum deserve a shot at chelation." (Chelation is the process of removing heavy metals from one's system via a chelating solution. One primary DAN! belief is that autism is caused by mercury poisoning.)

"All kids on the autistic spectrum have trouble releasing metals."

I listen nervously while Griffin wiggles in my lap.

I challenge him with a few questions. "Do you argue with the theory that autism is genetic?"

He answers, "I think the inability to process metals is genetic, yes."

"Isn't chelation dangerous? What about that boy Tariq who was killed during chelation?" I ask, referring to the tragic chelation therapy–related death of five-year-old Abubakar Tariq Nadama.

He shifts in his seat, clears his throat. Perhaps he's not used to parents' knowing things. He answers, "That was IV chelation, which we won't do here. Also, they used the wrong solution. You have to know what you're doing."

Eventually, he writes up a plan of action for Ezra. We'll start—judiciously, I note—with testing to see if he actually does have excess metals, yeast, or deficiencies. The assumption is that vaccines contain ethylmercury, and children with propensities to not release metals from their systems will experience neural damage. Various other mineral deficiencies may imply metals are wreaking havoc on his system. I pay my $250, plus another $200 in supplements, and gather the home tests that I realize will also need to be paid for when they're sent in, another $350 worth.

Next, we go to the room where they will take his blood. Ezra senses something bad is going to happen and starts whimpering. I hold him on my lap, Griffin in his car seat, while Ezra tries to wrench free. He screams with fear as they tie the rubber tubing onto his arm. The nurse, annoyed, says to me, "Can you hold his arm down, please?" I do. "And his legs, so he stops kicking me?" She doesn't make eye contact. Doesn't look at Ezra. He hollers with fear and pain as they stick in the needle. The blood seeps into the container slowly, and the nurse shakes her head. "We didn't get a good vein." I can barely hear her over Ezra's terrified screams.

"I don't care," I say. "This will have to be enough."

The nurse looks at me, still irritated. "We need a lot more blood for these tests to be done."

"We'll just have to do what we can."

She lets out a passive-aggressive sigh. *I know, I know,* I want to say. I'm a bad mom, a wayward mom. This isn't new. I don't do enough for him, or I do too much. I am never, ever doing the right thing. I feel this even now when I'm quite sure I'm doing right by

Ezra. This is the inadvertent evil of DAN! doctors and their staff. Surely they know how vulnerable we mothers can feel, how easily we will agree to whatever they say is the answer.

I take Ezra, who is hiccuping and gasping, exhausted, trying to feel better, trying not to cry anymore, and I buckle him into his car seat, and we go home. On the way, we stop at the store for some food. I put both boys in the cart, which always works best, and go to the deli. The man behind the counter is ridiculously attractive. His eyes are night-sky blue. His lips are heart-shaped. When he smiles at me I literally feel it in my pelvis. It's hard to look at him straight on. But I do, and I order a turkey and swiss on wheat.

"Those are some cute kids you got there," he says.

"You think?" I say. "I find them homely." I smile. If I could wink, I would do it in a second, but I have some sort of facial impairment that makes it so I've never been able to.

He laughs. "I don't know how they got so homely when they've got such a beautiful mother."

My whole body is lit up, that whole miserable mess with Dr. Destroyer a million miles away. "I'll bet you say that to all the women who come here wanting a turkey sandwich."

He laughs again, and I see his eyes go to my hand, my left hand, where my wedding ring is. It's too late to try to hide it. When my sandwich is ready he says, "Hope to see you again."

I just smile and turn away. I fear that if I speak, I will say something that reveals how desperate I feel.

four years old

Young Frankenmilk

That evening, Michael ignores me. I'm pissed about this, and tired. I just spent the better half of the afternoon trying to keep Ezra from throwing sand while he was in the sandbox with other children at the playground, and while the other moms gave Ezra and me dirty looks. Irritated by my nos, Ezra finally got up and found a patch of dirt in the gravel road that leads to the park and played with that. Okay, it's true that before this I had been flirting shamelessly with another man, but right now I can remember only the time at the park. Memory is selective when you want to be right.

Michael isn't doing anything wrong, per se. Rather, he's constantly being helpful, constantly cleaning, constantly moving. He carries laundry to the machines, sweeps floors, picks up toys. He never stops, always working, always moving, wearing that look of doom. This is how he deals with his misery. When Michael and I first met, he was all lightness, all pep. He was known wherever he went as the silly one, the guy who entertained. He'd break out into goofy dances. In regular conversation he is so quick-witted and hilarious, I have laughed hard enough to pee just a little in my underwear.

When we left Portland, his company put on two going-away parties for Michael, and they told me he would be sorely missed, that they expected their workplace to sink into numb dullness with him gone. Everywhere he went, in fact, people gravitated toward him. They asked me, "Is he like this all the time?" I'd tell them, "Oh, yes. Either he's like this or he's a miserable wet blanket." They laughed, perhaps not believing me. But the reality is that he has this other side to him, a dark part whose mother died when he was very young, whose stepmother was cruel to him, a part that he's never dealt with, that he's pushed deep beneath the surface.

Historically, he pushed his darkness down so far below that those wet-blanket times were spaced out enough to be bearable. Now, they are here just about every day. I feel sorry for him. I do. I know he's not good with change, considering the difficult changes he endured as a child. And here we've created as much change as anyone could in such a short time: We got married; had two children, one with special needs; moved across the country; sold and bought a house; and started a new job. He is sinking beneath it all.

If I'm going to be fully honest, I know this misery isn't solely about him. While he moves and moves and accomplishes tasks, he leaves behind him a wake of unexamined emotion. He is dealing with the physical world, yes, but I am left to navigate the emotional world, the thick sludge that fills the rooms. It is so much like my childhood, when I felt that no one was taking care of me, when no one contained me. And the danger lies there—in those childhood feelings. We're both adults, with children to care for, with a special-needs child, but I fear Michael and I are children ourselves in this way. I fear we're the ones with much more severe special needs. And

four years old

also, I need him. I desperately, desperately need him. We are the only two people in the world who can truly be there for each other regarding Ezra.

I can't focus on this, however, because tonight we have to figure out how to put three hundred different supplements into Ezra's milk, the only thing he drinks. No water, no juice, just the same daily mix of cow and rice milk. I pull them out of the bag: probiotics, enzymes, dimethylglycine, trimethylglycine, vitamin B_6, folinic acid, taurine, glutathione, cod liver oil, flaxseed oil, enzymes, and zinc. Don't ask me what half these items are supposed to do for Ezra. Dr. Destroyer explained them to me, but I've already forgotten. It's too much information to contain.

We already use a couple of these, like the cod liver oil and probiotics, but I bought a fresh supply from Dr. Destroyer's pharmacy because I think maybe his are better. Michael and I stare at the bottles and capsules, wondering how in the hell we are ever going to get these things into Ezra's body. Forget getting them into his body. How are we going to fit them into his milk? Lest we forget, we also have a new vitamin and mineral supplement I found online, of which he will need a full dose every day, and which has the added purpose of hiding any flavors from the other ones. To make the situation worse, Ezra will only drink out of a particular type of seven-ounce plastic cup, and only with the same spout on the lid. Not the light blue ones with the little textured grips on the side. God forbid.

Tonight is just the first night. We are daunted, to be sure. But over time we will have this down to a science. Ezra right now, when he is almost three years old, will ask, "More milk?" as he always does in the exact same way. (In the future this will transform into "Fresh milk." Then, at our insistence, "I want milk." Then eventually, "I want more fresh cold milk.") We will put on our imaginary lab coats and drop powders and liquids into his milk. A teaspoon of this, a sprinkle of that. We imagine the liquid gurgling, smoke flying up from his little plastic cup—*poof!* Allow me to present to you . . . Frankenmilk.

Tonight, though, Ezra watches us, making us nervous, and we screw up and put in too much of something too soon. Ezra examines the cup, twisting it this way and that, and finds the remains of some supplement in the spout. He makes a face and hands it back to us.

"More milk?" he says.

We pour some out, refill some milk, clean off the lid, and finally have the balance right. He goes off into the living room to look through a book. In a moment, he's back.

"Put it on?" he asks.

"Put what on?" I ask. I'm in the middle of making dinner.

"Put it on?"

"Put what on?"

"Put it on?"

I crouch down to his level. "Ezra, what do you want me to do?"

"Put it on?"

four years old

"Show me."

I follow him into the living room, where he takes a gulp of milk and then sits to read his book.

"Ezra," I say. "What do you want me to do?"

He ignores me, turning the page. Next he jumps up, smiling. He laughs, then sits back on his knees to turn to the next page. He hasn't looked at me once.

I shrug and go back to the dinner. A few seconds later, Ezra shows up again.

"Put it on?" he says.

Welcome, friends, to my life.

ON JULY 25, Ezra turns three. Two days later, he becomes violently ill. He dry-heaves, sleeps, moans, throws up. I call the pediatrician, who tells me there's a stomach flu hitting the one-, two-, and three-year-olds. After twenty-four hours, he should be done. She says, "When he's ready to take liquid, give him water, then move on to something with electrolytes, like Gatorade, and when he wants to eat, give him dry toast." I thank her, and hang up the phone. Explaining Ezra's eating habits is rarely worth it.

Twenty-four hours later, he's the same. He still vomits, and when he's not vomiting, he's just lying there. I call Michael and he comes home so we can take Ezra to the ER. Ezra's never been sick before, not like this. He's had a few colds, a few low-grade, uneventful fevers. Just once he had the stomach flu, but it lasted all of four hours, and between bouts he played. I fear he's dehydrated now, and that's why he can't get better. The intake nurse asks us a lot of questions, then takes us to a room and closes the curtain. Ezra tosses and turns on the hard, paper-lined bed, trying to be comfortable. I nurse Griffin, trying to keep him occupied. We wait and wait for a doctor. Finally, after almost two hours, one comes. He pronounces Ezra not dehydrated and gives him antinausea medication, which makes Ezra gag, and we leave. Over the next few hours he sits up a little more, plays with toys again, and asks for milk. I try to give him water, but he won't take it. Finally, he agrees to watered-down milk.

Of course, now that he is three, he receives no state-paid therapy unless we are willing to try school. I'm still undecided. The town where we live has an integrated preschool, which means that special-needs children are in class with typically developing ones. The teacher in charge has a degree in special education. Probably I should give it a try. This is always a difficult balance when it comes to Ezra. I don't want to hold him back. I don't want to underestimate him. But I also know he can't tell me why something upsets him, and his feelings deserve my respect, regardless of whether he has words to express them. The thought of him in a school, where people can judge him for his issues or assume things about him or misunderstand him, the thought of him away from the people who know him best, terrifies me.

Meanwhile, using the kits I received from Dr. Destroyer, I take

four years old

a stool sample (the details of which I'll spare you), pay the $85, and send the sample to a lab that will test for bacteria, overgrowth of candida, and the like. We also add DMSA to his milk for three days, collect his urine in little bags inside his diapers, and send in $225 to a different lab that will test for heavy metals.

SO MUCH OF the year has been laden with tests and worries and therapies that in August we try to focus on having fun. This neighborhood we live in is teeming with activities for kids—children's theater, museums, playgroups, and classes. I read them off to Michael and we glance at each other doubtfully. We disqualify some right off the bat. Sitting in a circle to listen to an adult talk? Cross it off. Can't bring in your own food? Cross that one off. A lot of children running around? Michael and I look at each other. That one's iffy. Sometimes Ezra doesn't care about a lot of erratic energy, sometimes he does. Cross it off. It's not worth the work of arriving there if there's a 50 percent chance we'll have to leave. Music involved? We laugh and cross that one off.

It's not that Ezra dislikes music. Not at all. Ezra's relationship with music is complicated. Few things stir him the way rhythm and melody can, and sometimes that stirring turns out to not be a good thing. When he was a baby, younger than a year old, he cried whenever a song ended or, after he learned the order of songs, which he always did, he cried when a CD ended. Once it played again, he was content. He calmed instantly if we spoke rhythmically, in a singsong voice. We were sure back then that Ezra would love baby sing-along and music programs, but with each one we took him to, all he did was cry. We would always leave early, full of apologies to the other parents, who watched us with expressions that made it clear they were glad to not be us.

Once, at a playground, I lifted Ezra into a swing. The little girl in the swing next to Ezra cried, and her mother, looking distraught, said, "I don't understand. She doesn't like to be swung. She cries every time."

I knew what it was like to feel worried about your kid, so I offered reassurance. "Kids are strange," I said. "It doesn't necessarily mean anything. This guy freaks out if someone starts singing."

She didn't make eye contact. "Well, she doesn't have *that* problem. She *loves* music." But that was long before I learned to stop talking to strangers about such things.

Over time we learned that Ezra doesn't like to hear music that is out of his control or out of the context of when and where he expected to hear it. New songs are usually acceptable. Songs he already knows well, songs they always play at children's events, like "Old MacDonald" or "Twinkle, Twinkle, Little Star," these songs send him into hysterics. Out of context, out of his control, they feel unexpected to him. Once, I had to leave a grocery store because a little girl was singing the "ABC" song. I also had to remove him from the pool, still soaking wet, when the swimming teacher played children's songs to make lessons more fun.

four years old

But he loves music intensely. He taps out rhythms in perfect sync. When he hears a song he likes, he wants to hear it again and again, memorizing it. There is little he doesn't love when it comes to music, although classical is by far his favorite. He loves music, but he needs to be in control of it, able to turn it on and off, or else he can easily become upset.

Michael and I whittle down our activity choices to the farm and the beach. Perfect. Nobody loves water, sand, or dirt more than Ezra. For today, we decide on the beach. We slather him and the baby with sunscreen, change diapers, gather cheese puffs, his cookies, and two premade Frankenmilks into a cooler.

Before we go, we watch Ezra dump the pieces from his alphabet puzzle and make words. He spells "pig," "cow," and "Ezra." Michael and I exclaim, "Ezra! You spelled 'pig'! 'Cow'! You spelled 'Ezra'! Look how smart you are!" He smiles at us, just briefly, and then puts the letters into a bucket to take to the beach. And we're off.

Here is Ezra: He digs his hands into the sand and watches as it pours through his fingers. He runs through the water, giggling. He takes fist after fist of wet sand and slaps it on his thighs, burying himself beneath it. He is so beautiful, my boy. Apple-round cheeks, shocking blue eyes, blond hair in the sun, chubby and pink, even without the food I so desperately need him to eat. I want Michael and me to be good enough for him. I want to keep him safe, keep him happy. I want him to love himself, with all his quirky ways and funny flapping arms, as much as we do.

He laughs and laughs as Michael chases him in circles. Then Michael picks him up. Ezra holds Michael's face between his two dimpled hands and gazes like a lover into his eyes. Michael carries him through the water, and Ezra looks out seriously at the vast lake, the sunlight broken and shimmering across it. I can't know what he's thinking. I can't know what will come, where he'll wind up. I can't know if he'll be loved, if he'll find some measure of success. He is my son, my everything, but he is not mine. He will grow in this world beside Michael and me. He will make his way. Somehow, somehow. We cannot save him from hard times. We cannot relieve him of pain. We will have to stand by, our arms useless at our sides, and simply watch.

With summer nearly over, Michael and I take advantage of the weather and try to spend as much time outside as possible. At least once a week until they close for the season, we put Ezra in his rain boots, pack his bucket full of plastic animals, and drive the twenty minutes to a farm that the owners have set up especially for children. They have a sand/dirt box the size of a small apartment, a rice table, water pumps, a playground, racing buggies, cows, pigs, sheep, goats, turkeys, rabbits, and chickens. One of the workers brings her teenage daughter, Angel, with her every day. Angel wears big red glasses and has acne that covers her entire face. She also has autism.

Whenever we arrive, Angel descends on us like an eager puppy. Griffin is still just a baby in a pouch on my chest, and she asks to hold him every time we go. When I tell her no, she pleads. She

four years old

asks incessant questions about Ezra and Griffin, tries to take Ezra's hand, and then picks him up without his permission. She hovers next to us, always too close, sticks her hands into whatever Ezra is doing, wanting him to be her friend. At some point, every visit, I wind up saying something to Angel, something straightforward and clear, something like, "That's enough, Angel. It's time to leave us alone now." She walks off and finds another family to annoy. It's part of the experience of the farm.

Whenever we go, Michael and I joke about how we are going to see Angel, but the truth is that I *am* going to see her. For all the ways she clearly struggles, for all the ways she doesn't understand social behavior, she seems happy. No one else seems to know how to handle her, but she is sure of herself. I like seeing that.

Facilitated Communication

Because my father commutes to consult at a company only forty-five minutes from our new home, he visits once a week. He arrives in time for dinner. My father is . . . well, he's an odd bird. In so many ways, Ezra is like my father, and his tendency toward obsession is one of them. When I was a teenager my father talked tirelessly about water heaters, which is what he designs at work. During dinner he would describe some feature of heat transfer that was causing a problem with a current design, or he would go on and on about a type of valve. Initially, I told him I didn't care. Then I yelled at him to shut up. Finally, I started taking my plate, standing up, and walking out of the room. He never seemed to understand that I wasn't interested.

When he visits now, twenty-plus years later, he does the same thing. He doesn't ask Michael or me about us, or if he does it is only to hear the raw facts, or to find out something related to his interests. If I leave the room for even a second, he speaks to twenty-year-old Nadine about issues at work. She smiles nervously, trying to be polite, until I walk back in there and wrangle him away. He talks endlessly about himself, saying unbelievably aggravating and embarrassing things like, "So what else about me?" Or, on seeing bananas in the fruit bowl, "I like bananas." He tells us about his day by saying, "Let's see, I woke up this morning, and then I went to the bank, and I said hello to the teller, who was wearing a pin that had a flower on it. . . . "

My father's inappropriate behavior isn't limited to his topics of conversation. He also doesn't seem to understand personal space. He sits on the arm of a chair my friend sits in so he can be close to her. He follows me around the house at my heels, telling me more about him. I used to think he behaved like this because he was insensitive and self-absorbed and didn't think enough of his own kids to ever listen to what we needed. But since Ezra's issues have shown themselves, I'm beginning to wonder if I've passed along my father's genetic tendencies. I have begun to think that my father might be right on the edge of the spectrum, with features of Asperger's syndrome.

His brother makes me wonder about genetics, too. He, unlike my father, dislikes being around people. As a child, my father's told me, my uncle was antisocial, spending most of his time in the basement performing experiments. Before he retired he made millions of dollars from inventing the sound systems that are now used by every major television station. Now he spends his time building and running steam trains and attending steam train conventions. Both my uncle and my father are engineers, and both are ridiculously intelligent. They can speak to each other for hours about some aspect of computer programming, isolating themselves from everyone else.

Tonight, before my father leaves, he goes to say goodbye to Ezra, who is watching a video. He stands in front of the television, blocking Ezra's view.

"Bye, Ezranoids," he says, his pet name for Ezra.

Ezra stands up and takes my father's hand. We all exclaim.

"Aww," Michael says, "You're taking Grandpa's hand, Ezra? That's so nice." But then Ezra walks my father out of the way of the television, lets go of his hand, and sits down again in front of the screen.

"Jeez," my dad says. "He's going to hurt someone's feelings by doing that."

I laugh, thinking he's joking, until I see from his expression that he's serious.

"Dad, he's *three*," I say. "If a three-year-old can hurt your feelings, I don't think Ezra's the one who needs help."

My father harrumphs.

"Besides, is it such a terrible thing? To not use up his brain space worrying about how other people feel?"

My father looks skeptically at me. He knows, as I do, that I have this trait, too. I'm thoughtful of other people's feelings, I'm empathetic, but I don't concern myself with worrying whether someone else's needs are being met, which I'm pretty sure is their own responsibility. It's not that I don't care what other people think of me. Unfortunately, I'm plagued by this worry too much. But I don't quiet my own opinions or emotions because I think it might make the other person uncomfortable. My blurting sometimes gets me into trouble, sure, but I've never known how to change it about myself. Over time, even though I've lost friends, even though people have steered clear of me, I've learned to like it about myself.

I know most autism specialists believe a desire to gain other people's approval is something Ezra needs to develop. I know why they think this. A lot of autistic kids want badly to make friends, but they don't know how to go about doing it. They assume Ezra is just like all autistic children. But he isn't. He's his own guy. And he's a guy who, at least for now, doesn't care that much about spending time with others. He's immensely self-contained. Is that the worst thing in the world? To decide he needs human relationships as badly as the rest of us do is presumptuous and arrogant. It suggests he has

four years old

to be similar to us to be happy. Meanwhile, I'm pretty sure Ezra is a lot happier than I am and most of the people I meet. Let's be clear: Ezra won't be like you. He won't be like me. He's always, always, always going to be only him.

And besides, when Ezra is a teenager and everyone around him is busy changing who they are so the popular kids will let them sit with them at lunch, maybe my son will be working out quadratic equations. Or he'll be drawing pictures. Or he'll be playing guitar. Or he'll do something else. Whatever it is, he probably won't be concerned with whether the other kids think he's worthwhile, or whether everyone else is happy, and that makes me glad.

AT THE BEGINNING of September, Ezra is sick again. It's surely the same virus as before. He sleeps, feverish, he wakes, vomits, moans, and sleeps again. He has a virus. He just has a virus. But it's hard not to worry, not just about how he will manage through this illness, but how he will manage through his life. It's hard not to let this smaller flu ripple out in concentric circles, as if the sickness were a stone dropped in a pond. He'll make it through this virus, and then what? And then what? And what then? His whole life waves out before me, a series of my fears, one after another.

I call Michael at work too many times.

"He's just sick," he tries to reassure me, working hard not to feel anxious. "Kids get sick."

Eventually, in a day or two, Ezra starts to sit up, play with toys, smile. Michael and I hug and kiss him, desperate to have him back. We remind ourselves how lucky we are that our son doesn't have a medical condition, that he isn't terminally ill, that he will likely be here tomorrow. We exclaim over his lovely smile and the way he laughs. How he dances and sings with the music. How perfect he is.

And then he does something: He smears his poop and wipes it in his hair. He walks out into the street while we yell, "Ezra, stop!" He sits in a pile of dirt and throws it, making clouds of dust in the air, ignoring us while we call, again and again, for him to come. I hold his arm, too tightly, and yell, "Stop touching your poop! Stop it! You're going to make yourself sick!" I yell, "What is wrong with you? Why can't you listen? Why can't you ever remember?" I fail him over and over again in this way. I lie in bed thinking of how I fail him. I'm not good enough for him, this small boy who needs patience, who needs understanding, who needs his parents to let him learn how he'll learn.

Nadine, I notice often, is all those things with him. She lies with him on the floor and helps him arrange alphabet letters. She draws him pictures of characters he loves. Sometimes, she leaves the baby with me and heads off to the swimming pool at the community center so Ezra can swim, one of his favorite things to do. I know what this means, because soon after she arrived, she let us know that water scares her. When she saw Ezra's joy, though, she forced herself to be in that pool so he could be, too.

four years old

School starts, and I decide to give it a shot. I can't shield him forever from other people. I can't deny him a chance to be in the world. We buy a Thomas the Tank Engine backpack and fill it with his necessities: a Frankenmilk, some cheese puffs, and a brief list of his phrases ("Come, Mama"), what they sound like ("Um, Ama"), and what they mean ("Help me"). It's our very own travelers' phrase book for Ezraland.

The school is small, off a winding country road, and the pre-school classroom has a separate entrance near a circular driveway, so you can park your car along the side of the drive and walk your child inside. I hold his hand and we head in. The teacher has already made clear to me that I am not allowed to stay. Neither is Nadine. It is her policy, part of her broad belief that parents are often overly protective, and that children should separate quickly, like removing a Band-Aid.

"Even if the child has special needs?" I asked.

"Yes," she said.

"Even if he communicates differently and a stranger might not know what he wants?"

Yes, even then.

The room is relatively large, with big rectangular tables for the kids to do work on. There are easels and shelves filled with books, drawers that have markers and clay and dinosaurs and cars. There's a dollhouse and a play garage, and a big pile of beanbags. Ezra runs off to a table with Play-Doh already out, and I take Griffin, who is asleep in his car seat, and walk out of the room, looking back a few times to see him involved. I take a breath, trying to be optimistic, trying to believe he'll be fine.

As soon as I'm back in the car, I call friends, my mother, anyone. I can't call Michael. I don't want to scare him. I don't want to send him down that spiraling path, worrying whether Ezra will be okay. We haven't spoken directly about our fears regarding Ezra. We can't. To do so might make them come true.

I park to buy a coffee and bagel. The day is cool and sunny. The many oaks and maples that line the streets are beginning to turn yellow, orange, and rusty red. Many of the people who live here originally hail from New York or Boston, like I do. I was sure when we moved here I'd slip back into my New Yorkness, but that hasn't happened. Instead, if people ask me where I'm from, I say Portland.

The woman who takes my order comments on Griffin's thick hair.

"You should see his brother's," I say. I know the moment that it is out of my mouth that I need to talk about Ezra, to keep him with me. This must be why, when she asks where Griffin's brother is, I tell her he's at preschool. His first day.

"Oh, mama," she says. "Don't worry. He'll be okay. They cry sometimes at first, but then they have so much fun. I bet he won't want to go home."

"But it's different for him," I say. "He's on the autistic spectrum."

She cocks her head with sympathy. "I'm so sorry."

"No," I say quickly. "No. There's nothing to be sorry about. He's an amazing person. He's loving and gentle and happy and so smart."

The woman looks uncertain. I'm one of those crazy women, I realize. I'm one of those people in the checkout line telling this stranger my life story while someone shifts around on his feet behind me, wanting to just order his bagel.

"Oh," she says. "Well, okay, then. They're all so precious." She smiles at Griffin as she hands me my bagel. "You take care of them."

I nod, duck out of there. In the car I wrestle with my feelings. I hate it when people say they're sorry about Ezra. Ezra is mostly an easy kid. He doesn't tantrum excessively. He doesn't run around like a madman, ripping things down off shelves, like I've seen plenty of typically developing kids do. But the truth is that sometimes I feel sorry for myself, for the ways I have to worry about who Ezra will be, how he will fare, in a different way from those people without special-needs kids. And for little things, such as how I can't take him to cafés where we can sit together and eat a treat and talk about the things on his mind, which someday I'll be able to do easily with Griffin.

When I pick up Ezra later, arriving early, his face is red and blotchy. He walks along the edge of the playground while the other kids squeal and play on the jungle gym. I take him in my arms and find the teacher, who is sitting on a bench, chatting with her assistant.

"Why does he look like he's been crying?" I ask.

She nods. "He had a rough day."

"Why?" I ask. "Why?" I try my hardest to stay calm, to not start crying myself, to not be the crazy, irrational mom I've already been today.

She shakes her head and gives me her best empathetic expression. "It's normal to have a hard first day. Lots of kids do."

I look at the other kids laughing and chattering on the slide. I take a deep breath.

"He'll be okay," she says. "I'll bet tomorrow is better."

But it isn't. And neither is the next day. On the fourth day, he whimpers when we pull up in front of the school, and I consider not taking him in at all. But I do, and somehow when I pick him up later, his day was fine.

The next week, he has another bad day. When I ask the teacher why, she tells me that he tends to cry when the whole preschool class walks, holding hands, down three hallways to go to the school's gym. I know my son. He doesn't know what the gym is, nor does he understand why he should have to go there. All he knows is that he's being taken away from a room full of toys and art materials and being made to walk down long, empty corridors. The teacher says, "He had a hard time going to the gym again today, but otherwise he did great."

I ask her, "Is it so essential that he go to the gym? Can't he stay in the classroom?"

four years old

She frowns, probably thinking, *Oh, here we go, another mother wanting special treatment for her child*, and says curtly, "We don't have enough staff for that."

Every day, I call Michael to tell him how it went. For both Michael and me, the mood of our entire day has begun to hinge on how Ezra's day is at school, which is too much responsibility to place on a three-year-old.

When Michael comes home from work, after we've gotten the kids to bed, we discuss the situation.

"If we take him out of the school, he won't receive therapy. Have you looked into private speech therapy?" he asks.

"Of course I have," I say. "There's nothing here."

Michael shakes his head, surely thinking, as I often do, of Patty, the fantastic speech therapist we left behind in Portland. "We never should have left Portland."

I sigh. I'm not sure we should have left either, but we have tacit agreements, as many couples do, to maintain balance. If he's going to take the we-never-should-have-left tack, then it's up to me to take the you-haven't-even-given-it-a-chance tack. It's how we keep ourselves from falling too far into dark and unknown places. It's how we protect each other.

"But we did leave Portland," I say. "And we made that decision together."

"I didn't say we didn't."

"But you're implying it's my fault, like always."

He turns on SportsCenter and doesn't look at me.

"So now you won't talk to me?" I ask.

"I just want to relax," he says. "I'm tired. I don't want to have a conversation right now."

I go upstairs and check on the baby, who is fast asleep. Then I check on Ezra, also asleep. I open my computer and poke around, until finally I settle on my email, where I write a note to Frank: *"Missing you. Would love to have another get-together. Would love to do anything other than this."*

Visual Spatial Skills

Ezra's tests results come back from Dr. Destroyer's office. His bloodwork reveals that he's sensitive to wheat and milk, but, barring removing the two items he eats and taking away the one way I have to ensure that he receives any nutrition—Frankenmilk—I can't do anything about this. A pediatrician told me long ago that I should just take away the food Ezra eats and replace it with broccoli and steak. Eventually, she told me, he'll eat it. I know from reading accounts of other children with severe eating issues that this isn't the case. Ezra will put mud and dirty leaves in his mouth, but he'd starve himself before eating something that makes him anxious. Besides, I'm afraid if I took away the food items he does eat that he'd refuse everything, and then we'd be in a situation where he

four years old

wasn't chewing anymore. More than one parent has said to me that they don't know how I can deal with this, which is easy for them to say. I'm not sure what choices I have otherwise.

Years later, I'll feel fine about my food choices for Ezra, since the gluten- and dairy-free diet—the most pervasive of alternative therapies for autism—is based not on any scientific substantiation, but on the theory of Kalle Reichelt, a Norwegian medical doctor and researcher. Reichelt believed he'd found a peptide in the urine of autistic and schizophrenic patients that resulted from an incomplete breakdown in wheat-based and dairy products. Since Reichelt's claims, several studies have not confirmed his original thesis. Still, we take Ezra off cow's milk and have him drink rice milk instead. We blend the rice milk into cow's milk gradually until we switch him all the way over to rice without incident.

We also learn from the lab report that Ezra doesn't have excess heavy metals. Thank God for that, since chelation, it turns out, is as dangerous as I suspected. Rather than remove metals from brain cells (which would be the only potential benefit of chelation, if indeed autism were caused by an excess of mercury), chelation releases metals into one's system, often sending them directly to the brain, as they also leave the body through urine. Along with the mercury go zinc, calcium, and other essential minerals we need to stay healthy. In fact, that little boy Tariq had cardiac arrest when the chelation—which also wound up being the wrong chelating solution—took so much calcium out of his body that it couldn't sustain his heart.

When scientific study after scientific study has shown again and again that thimerosal in vaccines is not responsible for autism, why would I even consider exposing my child to such dangers as chelation? Unless I were vulnerable enough—as I was at this time—to do anything a doctor said I should. Unless I felt afraid enough about what autism might do to our lives.

The test results do confirm Ezra's body has a tremendous overgrowth of candida. Dr. Destroyer prescribes the medication to treat the candida, which we add to Ezra's Frankenmilk for three weeks. Do we see a difference? Maybe. Possibly. He seems a little less irritable. He speaks a little more than before. Perhaps he's a little more comfortable. But he's still autistic.

All this DAN! doctor stuff pushes me to think more about the whole idea of Ezra's being autistic. Autism is not actually a thing. It's a constellation of symptoms. The questions I have are more about what causes his autism. Is it something outside of him, something that courses through his system like a virus, harming his real self? Or is it interwoven with the fiber of his being? And then, if it is an integral part of who he is, where is that line between helping him with the areas where the world feels hard for him and negating who he is?

Ezra didn't stop developing at some point. If I think back to who he was as a newborn, as an infant crawling around his playroom, he has always been who he is today. I'm beginning to see the danger that comes with trying to "remove" his autism. The danger is systemic, affecting not just his physical being, but also

four years old

what he will believe about himself as a human being, as a person with worth in the world.

I also think of my own needs in all this, because I should. Because my job as a parent is to clarify where I end and he begins. My parents didn't do that with me. They needed me to be more creative, more fun, the pretty one. They needed me to succeed, to not embarrass them, to put their feelings before my own. They needed me to reflect on them in a way that made them feel good about who they were. They needed me to be someone other than who I am. I won't, I will not, do that to my son. *That* is my greatest need: I must protect Ezra's self-esteem.

MOST DAYS, AFTER I drop Ezra at school, I drive and drive and drive, trying to understand where I am and how I fit into this foreign place. Griffin sleeps in the back. Although I know I shouldn't, I call Frank. Outside the oaks and maples stand lush and still against the road. The street winds and climbs over soft hills and curves. I let myself drift just a little. I let myself imagine it, just for a moment. It's just thinking. It's just imagining. What life might have been with Frank. Our conversations. The way he looks at me. The sex. It's silly to think like that, silly to even go there when the past doesn't matter anymore. What matters now is the future. What is to come. What *will* come? I have no way to know. Like most parents of a special-needs child, I worry about the future. I worry about who Ezra will be, what he'll be capable of.

This is why, driving through a town that day, I stop in and see a psychic. Do I believe in psychics? Not really. But psychics have crystal balls, and I desperately need one right now. Her name is Shannon, a black woman with tons of long braids. She wears layers of sheer, flowing material, like a black Stevie Nicks. She instructs me to take off my shoes and coat and to leave my purse near the door. "Bags," she tells me, "can pull the energy out of the room." I tell the skeptic in my mind to shut up, and I sit across from her. She asks me to close my eyes, breathe, and think about my main question. Then she tells me to pick some cards from her tarot deck.

"I have more than one question," I say.

"Put them in order of importance."

I take a big breath and begin with the biggest, the one that floats amorphously, following me wherever I go. The one that starts my day and ends it, that weaves through my daily choices and haunts my dreams—dreams about Ezra having a conversation with me, like any other boy—but a question that also means nothing, makes no sense if I try to pin it down. I tell it to her: "I need to know if my son will be okay."

"Tell me about him," she says.

Oh, now, okay. Hold on here. This is the thing about psychics. If she's so psychic, shouldn't she be able to tell *me* about him? This is how she's able to be "psychic," isn't it? She asks me questions, I tell her, and then, when she mirrors back what I've just said, I think, *Man, how does she know that?* But I reprimand my skepticism again, pushing it back into my brain. I decide to say the least amount possible. "He's not developing typically. He didn't start using words until he was almost two and a half."

She waits. When I say nothing more, she smiles. "You're not going to tell me more, are you?"

I shake my head.

She nods once. "I can work with that."

I raise my eyebrows, hoping she can. She flips over the cards I've chosen and studies them. I wait, my heart pounding. This is it. Whether I'm skeptical or not, she's going to answer the question. The Question. The one I live with day in and day out. Will my Ezra be all right?

"He's fine," she says finally, and I exhale. "He's not the one with the problem. It's everyone else who has the problem."

I nod, excited. This is what I believe! She's saying what I already sense! It's our society that pronounces Ezra disordered, a system of mental health that determines a clear line between people's neurology and defines whether a person is right or wrong. He has to fit this mold to be considered worthwhile, something I'm quite sure he'll never do. Ever since he was a baby, I've seen it happen, the way other people have been made to feel uncomfortable. He's never given them what they want. He hasn't cooed and smiled at them unless they've given him reason to. He hasn't needed their approval. He didn't make them feel good about themselves. Can confirmation from a psychic be all I need to change this for our family? Ezra is okay because there's nothing wrong with him to make him not okay. Can I just decide that this is true?

"Your son sees things the rest of us don't see. He doesn't have a need for the things many of us are limited by. He's here to teach us."

"Yes," I say, still excited.

"Tell me his name."

I tell her.

She shakes her head. "You must come up with a different name." I stare at her. She's completely serious. "That name is too heavy for him. It's too much weight to bear."

My stomach sinks. She's a psychic, a kook. Thanks for the reminder. "But that's his name," I say reasonably, as though this is something to have to explain. "We've been calling him Ezra since he was born."

I think of when Michael and I named him, this strange creature in my womb we didn't yet know. We didn't find out whether it was a boy or girl, but we hoped for a boy only because we loved the name we had: Ezra. We loved its phonetic sound, the buzzing z and hopeful a. It's an old Hebrew name, a character from the Old Testament who was a messenger for God.

"You must give him a nickname."

I hesitate. "Should we move on to my next question?" I ask.

She nods and shuffles the cards again. "Ask."

"My husband," I say, moving on to the next biggie.

"Name?" she asks.

"Michael."

She nods. Guess we won't have to worry about changing that.

"Pick three cards," she says when she sees I'm done talking. I do, and she flips them over. She stares.

"You've made the right choices."

"So, I'm supposed to stay with my husband?"

"Supposed to? Honey, there's no predestination. You make choices, and every choice is for good reason. Everything I tell you has great possibility. It is likely, but you could easily take a different path."

I frown.

"You don't like that, do you?"

"No," I say. "Not really. I thought the whole point of being a psychic was you could tell me what my future holds."

She nods and smiles. "Most people think this about psychics."

"So why am I paying you?" I ask, irritated. "Can I believe anything you just told me?"

"All I can do is tell you what my guides see, and my guides see where all the energy is pointing."

Energy, guides. I don't say anything more.

She smiles, seemingly reading my thoughts, which would be very psychic of her, I suppose. "You don't want to, but somewhere in there you believe."

"I'd like to."

"Go easy on yourself," she says. "This is your biggest obstacle in life. You demand too much of yourself. Your husband, too, I see. He needs to stop flogging himself. Both of you need to give yourselves breaks."

This is true.

"What is, is. Let it be."

She's right. I know it the second she says it. This is the answer. It's always the answer. It's part of every Eastern philosophy, every religion. Allow my life. Allow who Ezra is. Allow the fact that I both love and can't stand Michael lately, that I feel scared about our marriage. Allow that nothing has turned out the way I expected, the way I assumed it would back when Michael asked me to marry him and, in love, hopeful, thrilled, I said yes. I can feel the salvation, the sinking into my life. Stop the running. Stop holding tightly to what isn't there.

Tactile Defensiveness

The next time I see Frank, I meet him for a few hours in the same city where Ezra and I came to see Dr. Destroyer. He makes me lunch in his friend's studio loft. I have Griffin with me again. He sleeps on my lap while I watch Frank at the stove. Ezra is home with Nadine. Do I think of him? Of course I do. Ezra is always on my mind. He needs me, I know. So does Michael. So does Griffin. What do I need? I'm not sure yet. I map out the pros and cons in my head:

four years old

PROS:

> –Frank is a painter, which is very sexy.
>
> –Frank and I can talk for hours about art. Also sexy.
>
> –Frank likes most everything I say.
>
> –Frank thinks I'm cool.
>
> –Frank wants to have sex with me.

CONS:

> –Frank is married.
>
> –I'm married.
>
> –I have two children.
>
> –One of my kids has autism.
>
> –I'm an immoral jerk and a shitty mother.

I want to be better than this.

In the midst of my thoughtful analysis, Frank glances at me and says, point blank, "I'd like to have sex with you right now." He moves from pot to pan, sprinkling salt, then pepper.

I look down at Griffin, who is asleep, thankfully not a witness to the conversation. "I'm going to pee," I say. I stand up and walk to the bathroom. I look in the mirror and try to collect myself. I stare at my face. Am I one of those mothers who has sex with strange men while her baby sleeps nearby? Am I a mother who has reached the point of breakdown, perhaps, when everything changes and a new life starts rolling headfirst down a hill? Is this the answer, to just unravel? To give up?

"It's not going to happen," I tell Frank when I come back.

He smiles. "I didn't really think it would."

He serves the food onto plates and sets them on the table. Griffin wakes up and sits on my lap. He reaches for the shiny spoon. I offer him little mashed pieces of sweet potato, which he mostly refuses. He pads at my chest, wanting to nurse.

"I guess you're going to see my breasts one way or another this afternoon," I say to Frank, amused at how I make jokes when situations become tense.

When it's time to go, I buckle Griffin back into his car seat.

Frank stands, waiting for me to be done. "Can I at least have a hug?"

We press against each other way too closely. I can feel the hard warmth of his chest, the pressure of his hips. He pushes his head into my neck.

"You smell so good," he whispers.

Oh God. A wave of anxiety ripples through my body and I untangle myself, but we stand a moment, holding hands and looking at each other. It is impossible not to feel guilty, even now, recalling this. And yet it's just a hug, just a hug. Nothing is happening, not really.

EZRA'S FAVORITE ACTIVITY is splashing in the indoor swimming pool at a local community center. He goes often with Nadine, one of the few promises you can offer that will make him gather up his bucket of animals and letters and books and happily take your hand to leave. Sometimes he says, "Pool!" when we're in the car, hoping we can go. I show him a picture Nadine gave us of the two of them in the locker room. Ezra's grin in the picture is huge. He points now to a door in the background of the photograph.

"Open," he says.

"Open?" I ask.

"Open door."

I laugh. Does he think it's possible to open the door in the photo so that he can go play in the pool? Sometimes his different way of thinking catches me off guard.

Ezra also loves the museum we find nearby. It's an eclectic museum, with an aquarium in the basement, dinosaurs on the next floor, and art on the next. He likes the room with the fishes, the whole floor lit by blue light. He runs from one tank to another and points at the fishes' iridescent colors. Griffin laughs, watching Ezra. Few things delight Griffin the way Ezra can.

The discomfort I have about his school is always there. I want him to learn, I want him to gain social skills, I want him to be successful. He goes three days a week, his warm little hand soft in mine as I bring him into the room. I hug him goodbye and leave, afraid as always of what I'll find when I return. There is a girl in his class, Mary, who gives him hugs. She forces him to take her hand as we walk the children out to the cars at the end of the day. She says to her mother, "*I'll* take Ezra to his mama's car," and whether her mother wants her to or not, she pulls Ezra along, saying, "Come on, let's go. Time to go home. Come on, now." At the car, I lift Ezra and buckle him into the seat. When Mary's mother says, "Say goodbye to Ezra," Mary says, "Bye, baby," in her husky voice. I'm delighted by anyone who cares for my boy in this way, who can't help but love and nurture him. He's still small and cute, but his nature is so sweet, and this is likely what makes Mary act like his mama. She makes me believe there might be people like that—other than Michael and Griffin and me—who will love him, who will want to keep him happy and cared for.

I meet with Ezra's teacher, the special-needs director, and the therapists at Ezra's school for his IEP, which stands for individual education plan. All children who have special needs and attend public school must have one. Ezra is taken from the classroom twice a week for one-on-one speech therapy sessions. Once per week the therapist pulls a few other children from the classroom for a speech therapy group. An occupational therapist observes him once a month, which, as you might imagine, doesn't help him learn to eat.

In the meeting, the occupational therapist tells us the same thing we hear from every OT: "Sit him with you for meals; put one unacceptable food on his plate each time; give him an 'all done' bowl into which he puts the food he won't eat." I nod, as I always do, knowing full well none of these exercises will assuage his severe anxiety about eating. The speech therapist discusses how frustrated and confused he was for the first couple weeks when she took Ezra out of the room, but

four years old

now he's adjusted. She's working, as we are, with ways to encourage him into the back-and-forth of a conversation. He's talking now, but he doesn't nod his head or say yes, and he rarely seems to understand how to answer questions. Most of his speech is chunked and echolalic, imitating either videos or phrases we've said to him again and again. For Ezra, speech and its many rules for communication come at a crawl, hard-won. This therapist's idea is to have him mimic her responses when other kids ask him things. A boy says, "Ezra, do you want a turn?" And she looks at Ezra. "Okay." He repeats her: "Okay." It seems like a smart idea, but over time we'll learn that it, like so much else, doesn't make much difference.

And his strengths? I always have to ask. What is he doing well? They hesitate. They're so focused on his failings. I prompt them, "I know he's got exceptional spatial skills."

"Oh, right," one therapist says. "That's true."

But that's as far as we get, and our time is up. I stand, my chest tight with this familiar grief.

The lead teacher chats with the speech therapist on the way out. I catch a few sentences. She says with a cruel laugh, "I'd take a Hannah over a Mary any day." Hannah is another little girl in their class, quiet and well mannered. I pretend I don't hear, but I do, I do.

THANKSGIVING WEEK, EZRA is sick again with that flu. He vomits, sleeps, moans. This one is worse than before. For five full days we don't see him smile. He's so sick that he willingly drinks small sips of water, only to vomit them back up. I pace the house, fretting, trying to keep Griffin, who always wants to be with Ezra, away from him. I buy him a *Charlotte's Web* video, the 1973 version, with Paul Lynde's voice for Templeton the rat. It's the version where they talk about killing Wilbur for meat while the father carries an axe with which to do the deed. Michael and I find it amusing in this era, when the Cookie Monster is eating fewer cookies and more fruits and vegetables as part of an initiative to foster healthy eating habits in kids. I buy it to take Ezra's mind off feeling ill, and he watches it over and over and over and over again. He especially loves the songs. We take him to the doctor, where he lies in my arms moaning, wrapped in a blanket, pale, pale, my precious little boy. The doctor does nothing for him. No one ever does anything for him. I can't help but feel whiny like this, as though no one will ever understand. Finally, the day after Thanksgiving, Ezra comes back to us again. He sits up. He looks at a book. He smiles.

The teacher hands out progress reports. Here is Ezra's: Every last item is given the lowest possible mark, which is called optimistically *emerging*. I page through it, sick to my stomach, so confused. "Counts to five: *emerging*." "Recognizes at least three letters in the alphabet: *emerging*." Ezra counts to two hundred. I've seen him recite the numbers as Nadine writes them on the blackboard wall in the playroom, He's known all his letters since he was two and a half. The guy is spelling and reading a few words, for God's sake.

Are they out of their minds? Am I? I ask the teacher at his next class how they could have missed this.

She answers sharply, "He doesn't show us he knows those things when we ask him."

Then, just a few days later, I arrive to pick him up, still early, always early, and there he is on the playground with the other children. He walks along the edge of the sandbox, wearing his backpack. Ezra can't put on his own backpack. He's never done so in his life. None of the other children wears their backpack. Can you see this? Can you picture what I saw that day? They put his backpack on him, as if he were a coat rack, a *thing,* so it wouldn't be forgotten. Am I overreacting? Maybe. But when it comes to my child, there can't be second chances. Sometimes all we have to go by as mothers are our instincts. So I take him by the hand, I put him in the car, and we never, ever go back.

I HATE THAT I never have ease. I hate that while other mothers are easing through decisions for their child, are making holiday cookies and worrying over whether the snow boots are too small, or whether it's time to move out of the crib and into a big-boy bed, I pore over schools within driving distance, trying to find one where my son can belong. I look for supplements and approaches to try to encourage my son to eat food. I lie in bed and wonder how my son will ever be okay in the world, how I can ever help him love who he is and have his needs met. I can never be easy. I can never be still.

Always, I must be running, moving, searching, finding. Always, I am fighting against the unbearable default of failing my son.

I can't live like that all the time, immersed in my experience as a mother to my special-needs son, so I set up a meeting with my agent and editor. On a Tuesday morning, I wake early, put Griffin into his car seat, leave Ezra with Michael, and drive down to Manhattan. I'm looking forward to the drive, during which I can just relax and feel excited about meeting my agent and editor in person for the first time. For just a few hours I want to think about something other than what's happening with Ezra or what's happening with my marriage.

Twenty minutes into the trip, Griffin starts screaming. I try talking softly to him. I try singing to him. I pass him toys and a bottle with water and baby biscuits. Finally, I can't stand to hear him so distressed anymore, so I pull into a rest area and nurse him, hoping he'll fall asleep. He doesn't. As soon as I put him back in his seat and sit back in mine, he starts fussing, louder and louder, until he is full-on screaming again. It goes on for so long that I pull over again, worried that he's in some kind of pain. I change his diaper, check for a rash, and double-check his penis (since I once read on some message board that a hair could wrap around it and squeeze, causing pain). I check his ears to make sure they aren't red. I examine each of his little fingers and toes. I feel for fever, check the pajamas he's wearing to make sure no tags are scratching at him, press my fingers around his seat to see if anything might be poking him.

Everything seems fine, so I put him back in his seat and we take off again. Of course, he begins to scream once more.

I once read that some parents put earplugs in their ears while driving with infants and toddlers so their crying doesn't stress the driver out too much, and I thought I could never do such a thing because I'd want instead to do something about the crying. But right now I understand. We have about 160 miles more to drive, and I've barely made progress because my infant—who has everything I can think of to give him and who has nothing I can find hurting him—won't stop yelling.

After another good half hour of his screaming, he falls asleep. He was just tired. Unbelievable, this kid. But at least the rest of the drive is silent and I feel like I can breathe. I arrive at my father's apartment in New Jersey, which is where I plan to keep the car, and my father drives us to Midtown. When we arrive, I stuff Griffin into his sling and we walk toward the restaurant. Griffin is excited and wide-eyed, babbling and exclaiming. He seems to like the hustle and bustle of the people all around.

When we arrive, the hostess leads us to the table where my editor and agent already sit, and for a glorious hour I am able to focus on my work with two other people who want the best for my book as well. Of course, somewhere in there I have to nurse Griffin, which means both my agent and my editor wind up catching a glimpse of my boob. And of course, at some point Griffin takes a dump, which means I have to change him on the hard bathroom floor in the tiny bistro bathroom while horrified New Yorkers step around us. But it's all worth it.

Afterward, I meet Frank in Central Park. We've agreed it won't be for long. He's in town for his own purposes, so why not meet for a bit and chat? I wear a black miniskirt and Frye boots, and I catch him checking me out as I approach. It's nice to see him, but also it's cool to have someone to talk to about my lunch. I want to revel in it for a little bit, rather than fall right back into the muck of my life. We talk about my lunch and his art while Griffin crawls around on the grass. After a while, he settles in for nursies and falls asleep, and then it feels like it's just Frank and me, which is both enjoyable and nerve-racking.

When I drive up to Massachusetts later that afternoon, we talk on our cell phones and discuss what we would have liked to do to each other. To talk with Frank with such abandon about sex is dangerous, but also so entirely removed from my real life it's like talking about unicorns. In just a few hours, I'll be back home with Ezra, and with my husband and the distance that sits between us like a cavernous hole.

A FRIEND FROM Michael's college days visits. A family. Their youngest child, a happy, sweet little girl who is almost two, was born premature and still can't walk. Their developmental pediatrician suspects cerebral palsy. In a moment when it is just the girl's mother and me, cutting up fruit for a salad, she explains to me what

four years old

they've gone through—the therapies, the diagnoses, the surgeries—and she says, shockingly, without looking at me, "Sometimes I wish we never had a second one." My breath catches. I say nothing. Such a brave, human thing to say. I know she doesn't mean it the way someone else might hear it. I know she loves her daughter as fiercely as any other mother loves her child. But I understand the need to tell someone, to say something hideous. The need to say this truth and have the listener understand. In the future, I'll make a new friend, a mother to an autistic boy who needs a lot of hands-on help, who has a piercing scream when he doesn't get his way and is still in diapers at age six. She will say, "Autism ruins my fucking life. I wish I could say that and not be misunderstood." Being misunderstood is pretty much the number one experience for parents like us.

A year later, another mother I know of from an online special-needs parenting board will lose her severely autistic child to a grand mal seizure. She addresses that terrible question that must come up: *Am I just a little relieved? No*, she writes. *I wished for it sometimes, I admit. But now that it's happened, the hole in my life, in my heart, is too big. I feel lost without him.* As though she would love her son less because he's disabled in some way. As though it is less of a tragedy for an autistic child to die. As though a parent can live in a world that doesn't hold her children, regardless of who or what they are.

Michael's friend's son is just a little younger than Ezra. He jumps and squeals on a mattress we have on the floor of our family room, meant for exactly that. Ezra joins him and they jump, jump,

jump, laughing and chanting together, "Jumping on the bed, jumping on the bed." Kids are so good at that, being inside their joy. We laugh with them, trying to learn.

Broken-Mirror Theory

Michael and I make our way through the winter holiday. The snow has been falling, one snowstorm after another, burying our house, burying us, burying our lives under its soft blindness. Our front door is shut tight, trapped behind a snowdrift. I don't want to be here. I don't want to be anywhere. I just want us to find a way to live through this, for my son to be okay, for my family, somehow, to be okay.

I drive with the boys to visit my friend and her two little girls. I both adore and can barely stand her older daughter, who is a few months younger than Ezra.

"Look at my beautiful dress," she says.

"I see it," I say, resentment rising into my throat.

"Do you think it's beautiful?"

"Yes," I tell her. "I do." I stand up from the couch quickly and leave the room, aware that I'm about to cry.

My friend follows me, worried.

"No, no," I say, shrugging her off. "Really, I'm fine."

"You sure?"

four years old

"Yes," I say. I smile and brighten. "Totally fine."

I do this. I won't let anyone see what I'm really feeling, not my kind friend, not Michael. I won't even show the full extent of it to myself. If I did, it would mean giving power to my grief. It would mean that while Michael was slipping further and further down his own slope of despair, I would join him. And then who would take care of the children, of us? Who would keep this family alive?

Michael starts therapy, and so do I. Michael's therapist pronounces him depressed and starts him on an antidepressant right away. My therapist lets me examine my feelings about Michael. He says, "You expect too much of yourself."

I say, "Really? I have a son with autism. And a baby."

"You're also just a person, like anyone else, who wants to be loved."

I look at the blue and red patterns in the rug on the floor and then out the window, at the black trees and white mantle of snow. Above us, someone walks across a room. My therapist works in an old house, the kind with a sweeping staircase and stained-glass windows. And also the kind it must take thousands of dollars a year to heat.

"But I already did this," I tell him. "I wrote a whole book about how I spent a decade and a half disallowing intimacy. I've gained the insight, done the work. What is wrong with me that I'm back to square one?"

He smiles. "I don't know. Maybe life is tough right now, and maybe it's hard to be on top of things when life is tough. Maybe you're human."

I don't smile back. It would be easier, perhaps, if I had a diagnosis. Depression, like Michael. A personality disorder. It would be easier to just name it, to know what is wrong with me, why I can never figure out how to be happy, present, just living my life. But I know this psychologist's assessment is probably correct. My diagnosis is that I'm human, and of course there's no cure for that.

Michael's therapist is a different sort of guy. Michael tells me his therapist, whom I shall call Dr. S, has invited me to join him at a session, since depression is usually a couples' issue. So I leave the kids with Nadine and go. Dr. S arrives late and apologetically, carrying a pile of files and loose papers and a briefcase. He's dressed in a jacket and tie, a tacky one.

"Sit, sit," he says. I sit on the couch, and when Michael sits in the chair across from me I look at him like he's crazy.

"Aren't you going to sit next to me?" I ask.

"Why?"

And then Dr. S sits behind his large desk, and I understand. This guy sees patients from *behind his desk!* I look back at Michael, wishing I could send him some secret message about this, something letting him know that I think his therapist is from the dark ages.

"I wanted you to know that Michael is very depressed," Dr. S says to me, jumping right in.

four years old

I nod. I know that. It's why Michael is so miserable all the time. It's why he always tends toward negative thinking, is always stuck in a downward spiral. It's largely why we don't have sex. Sometimes I think Michael married the wrong woman, that he needs someone with more resources than I have, someone who will simply love him through his depression, without needing any-thing back. Don't such women exist? Women who say things to their partners like, "I'm here for you, through thick and thin. You take your time. You go off to sea, into your cave, away from me, and I'll be here when you come back." It's what women are sup-posed to do, aren't we? We're supposed to stand by our men, no matter what their damage.

Dr. S stares at me, perhaps not believing that I understand.

I glance at Michael, uncomfortable, and see that he's bouncing his knee, fidgeting, tapping his fingers against the chair's arm.

"Why don't you tell me a little bit about what's been hard for you concerning Michael?" Dr. S asks. He rests his bearded head in his hand, prepared, it looks like, to listen.

So I tell him. I tell him about the lack of romance and sex, the distance, the silence, the grudging way he seems to do anything that involves his family.

Dr. S nods, sometimes making faces of delight or disgust that make no sense to me. I talk quickly, sensing from Dr. S that he is dying to get a word in. Finally, he breaks in.

"Let me tell you something you need to hear. You need to

stop treating this guy like you know what's best for him, like you're his mother," he says, in an *I*-know-what's-best-for-*you*-though manner.

I lean back into the couch. This isn't my first encounter with such a therapist. I was actually trained to be this sort of therapist. I mean, I was trained to listen (new therapists are actually taught behaviors to make it *look* like they are listening). But I also learned to take stock of people and then tell them what they needed to do—ridiculous ideas, like pros and cons lists and starting to exercise. Hadn't they already thought of those things themselves? Weren't they in a therapist's office because while they knew the basics of what they needed to do, they couldn't seem to accomplish those things on their own? Why do some therapists treat their clients like dogs in a canine obedience class?

I glance again at Michael, who is still so anxious he looks like he might jump out of his skin. Dr. S is too caught up in his lecture to notice. The hour continues like this, with Dr. S telling me, and sometimes Michael, what we need to do to be happy together. When we leave, not soon enough, Michael looks at me, wincing a bit.

"I need a new therapist, don't I?" he asks.

We walk outside without saying much of anything, and drive away in separate cars.

I SPEND MUCH of the afternoon on the phone with Frank, trying to distract myself from the strains of my marriage, the growing

four years old

distance I feel with my husband, the fear I always have about what I am or am not doing for Ezra.

Frank says, "I had an idea today about where we should live."

I'm doing my best to keep Griffin busy with the train table so he doesn't wake Ezra from his nap. I smile now. Frank and I are always in fantasy mode. "Tell me," I say.

"They have apartments for married couples who teach at the school," he says, referring to the university where he teaches art. "I'll get you a job here."

"We won't be married," I say. I am well aware we spend too much time hashing out details about things that will never come to pass anyway. We do this often about having a baby together. He thinks it's something he might like to do. I know I don't. But we discuss it anyway, like it's a real issue between us, like it isn't the absolute last thing we need to be worrying about.

"I'm sure you don't have to present a marriage certificate," he says.

I move a train closer to Griffin so he can reach it. "What about my children? Where will Ezra go to school?"

"We have one of the best childhood development centers in the country."

He has a point.

"Is there a yard for them to play in?"

"The whole campus is a yard," he says.

"Okay."

Then we are both quiet, aware we're talking about nothing.

When I'm not distracting myself with Frank, with the fantasies I attach to him, I try to distract myself in other ways. Often I sit at my computer, searching for something, anything, that will make me feel better. It's so silly to look for connection on the Internet, in this odd unreal world, so stupid to look for answers. But what I find is a message board of special-needs parents. I don't relate to all of the parents there, but I do feel connected to some.

I begin to share my concerns about Ezra, about how I just want to accept him as he is, how I want him to be happy, to love life. A lot of parents, I learn, feel the same way. A lot feel those same hazy pressures that I do: We must do everything we can to make our children normal, to do something fast during the compressed "window of opportunity." A lot, like me, want to ignore this notion that there is a brief window in which our children can be helped, but we are afraid to. We're afraid our instincts might be wrong. We're afraid that we really are failing our children if we don't follow the path handed to us, one where all autistic children must participate in forty hours of behavioral therapy every week, receive chelation, and be made into something other than who they are. These parents have stores of information to share. They have links and researched evidence and book recommendations that help me build my own beliefs about what I should and should not be doing for Ezra.

I come to believe, for instance, that forty hours per week of any therapy for a child like Ezra would be more stressful than useful, at

four years old

least at this young age. I believe it is a dangerous assumption that all children on the spectrum would need the same treatment when, in reality, children are so different from one another in their abilities and challenges and behaviors. I believe some children might be harmed by vaccines or environmental pollutants, and other children, such as Ezra, were from the start who they are today and will be in the future. I believe random things happen in utero as a fetus develops, things no one could have predicted or done anything about, that lead to autism. I believe it makes no sense to argue that one cause or another leads to autism, because each family's experience is so utterly personal. I believe, as I always have, that our stories help one another, even as they are different in all of these ways.

I learn that not everyone feels like I do. Some parents spent the better part of a year demanding that someone recognize that their child was different, that they weren't just dealing with behavioral problems, that they didn't just need to discipline their children more. Some had knocked down doctors' doors, begging for referrals to specialists. Some had received misdiagnoses or dangerous advice. Many had been dismissed as overreacting.

Some people believe adamantly that vaccines led to their child's autism, that despite plenty of studies showing no link between vaccines and autism, they hold fast to what they know is true about their children. Some need this. They need an explanation, something to blame, something perhaps to obsess about to stay away from the grief about their children that would otherwise consume them.

Some people I meet online are autistic themselves. When I share that it is painful for me to feel like I can't understand how my child thinks, that there are so many times when I don't know how to provide him with what he needs, one mother writes back that this is exactly how she feels with her neurotypical children.

All parents are flawed because they, we, are just people. Some judge each other for not seeking evaluations, or for pursuing bio-medical treatments, or for not wanting their child to be autistic. Yet it's outrageous to judge any parent for their feelings, their convictions, for the ways they've found to cope with this alien world of being a special-needs family.

There are parents out there who have killed their autistic children. Parents of neurotypical children have committed patricide, too. The common denominator is not autism, it's pathology. Still, those stories enrage me because they are so sensationalized, because the media *do* make it about the autism and not the psychosis, because they encourage that notion in our society that autistic people are untenable, empty shells, that autism steals children from parents like the Devil might. Indeed, one of those murdered children was killed during an exorcism, when the preacher performing the exorcism pressed his knee into the eight-year-old's chest until he stopped breathing.

Even Autism Speaks, an organization that is supposed to be working for people affected by autism, ran an ad called "Autism Every Day." The mother in the ad infamously said in front of her

four years old

autistic daughter that she contemplated killing them both. The intention was to encourage people to donate more money to the research-based organization. There is nothing wrong with a mother's having intense, difficult feelings, but it is terribly disrespectful of Autism Speaks to use her feelings in an effort to raise money. For this and so many other reasons, Autism Speaks has become known among the neurodiversity community as "Autism Speaks Doesn't Speak for Me."

There are also the outsiders who come to visit the special-needs parenting board. They jump on to ask, "What's wrong with my neighbor's kid? I figure you guys will know. All he does is spin in circles and once he hit my daughter. Just curious." Or, "My friend's kid is obviously autistic because she won't look at me when I walk in, and my friend is so obviously in denial." These visitors enrage us. They turn us into unpleasant, nasty posters to whom the visitors always say, "It was just a question, jeez. You're all so oversensitive. I'll remember not to come back here again."

One of the mothers on the site contacts me by email off the boards. She likes the things I say there, and she sees from my website I'm a writer. Her son is recovering from brain surgery to have a tumor removed. She and her husband went through hell during the many months and litany of evaluations and testing it took to figure out what was keeping her son from developing his gross motor skills. When they finally found the tumor, she felt relief, terror, and intense guilt for not finding it earlier.

We exchange a few emails, learning a little more about each another. In a few years, I'll have a community of friends who also have special-needs kids. But here in Massachusetts, I have no one like that. More and more, I struggle to connect with parents who have only typical children. Sometimes I feel dumbly angry at them; sometimes I envy them, like I do my friend with her two girls. It would be nice to have some friends with whom I could just relax, could just feel how I feel about my family and say it and be understood, like Michael's friend knew she could that day. So I eagerly engage this woman.

Then, a few weeks into the friendship, I write something to her about how sometimes I think I should have a CT scan done for Ezra, just in case there's something there. I say how her story is a good reminder that you never know. She writes back, "Thanks for clarifying that you think I'm a bad mother."

I let her know I would never think that, and then I remove her from my email list.

Least Restrictive Environment

Now that Ezra's not in preschool, I have to find a speech therapist for him. Again. I have to keep moving, keep doing, I have to hurry up, hurry, hurry up. I have to help him before it is too late. I call the school system and find out he's entitled to therapy even if he doesn't attend the school. No one told me this. No one gave me this option earlier, which I might have chosen from the start. I might have saved him—and myself—from that harmful preschool experience. I understand that the school system can't be on top of everything. I understand the personnel are swamped with other matters. Still, I can't help but feel frustrated.

I take Ezra for therapy the following week. Icy snow sits on the edges of the parking lot. Mountains of snow pile on the walk. I try to make it fun, try not to let him feel my stress, once again, about seeing someone new. "Crunch, crunch, crunch," I say as we walk, quoting from one of his books. He looks up and smiles. "Crunch, crunch, crunch," he repeats.

The therapist assigned to Ezra wears heavy makeup. She reeks of perfume. She walks us into a tiny room with a desk and just a few toys. She says, "We'll just do some testing to see where he's at first."

I center myself. I try not to lose it. "Why does he need testing when he's been receiving services already through the school system? You can't read the file?"

"I'd feel more comfortable getting a sense of where he's at."

Right, and we wouldn't want *her* to feel uncomfortable.

She says words, and he's to repeat them. He understands this, and he does so, but after about five words, he doesn't want to anymore. I pull him onto my lap.

"Come on," I tell him. "Just a few more. You can do it."

Next, she shows him a series of pictures. "Where does the bird live?" she asks, emphasizing the "where." Ezra looks at the images, but he doesn't respond.

"Ezra," I say. "Where does the bird live? Which one?"

He points angrily at the nest. "Nest!" he yells, irritated.

She flips the page, and there is a picture of a boy and girl running. "Where is *he?*" she asks him.

"Ezra," I say, when he doesn't answer. He whimpers. "Where is *he?*"

"Running!" he yells, frustrated, and he points to the boy. I'm surprised. I didn't know he understood pronouns. There's so much I don't know about his skills, because they come so erratically. Sometimes I say things to him and he looks at me blankly, seemingly not understanding. Other times, he responds immediately by doing what I've asked. Also, when he knows things, he usually isn't interested in showing us.

"I actually need to ask him the questions in the exact way the manual instructs," she says. "He can't have your help."

Ezra is wiggling off my lap. He's on the verge of being extremely upset.

"Let me ask you," I say. "Does it really matter, in the broad scope of things?"

"I'm sorry?" She tries to remain pleasant, but her jaw twitches.

"Let's say you get skewed results on this evaluation." When I say "skewed," I make little rabbit ears in the air with my fingers. "In the end, do you honestly believe it will matter in terms of helping him?"

four years old

She eyes me, her jaw still jumping.

"I'm not trying to be difficult," I say. "I just want my son to receive support with his speech. And every time, he has to be evaluated, which stresses him out. And me."

"We want to do the best we can for him," she says.

"I realize that."

"We have protocol we have to follow . . . " she continues, but she trails off as she watches Ezra, who has gotten off my lap and is now flapping his arms with excitement because he's found a toy barn. "He flaps his arms," she says.

"That's true," I agree.

"You do know this is a sign of autism."

I stare at her, disbelieving. "And?"

"A child with autism needs lots more than speech therapy."

I start to gather my stuff. She watches me, disapproving, but I do my best to ignore her now. "Ezra," I call. "Let's go." Ezra takes my hand and we walk through the doorway of her little room. "Bye," he says.

"Okay, then," she says, completely missing my energy. "I'll call you to set up Ezra's appointments."

The next day, I split my time between writing and searching for a new school for Ezra. Michael and I agree that if he doesn't have any therapy, then he will at least have to be in school. It was never my plan for him to be in school so young, but if he has nothing—no therapy, no school—I feel like I'm failing him. I must do something do something do something and I must do it fast, before it's too late, too late.

Many people say Montessori schools are a great fit for kids on the autistic spectrum because they allow the children to follow their interests, they tend to require less social ability than other schools, they are often devoted to facts rather than imaginative play, and they have set rules about how to use the lessons. I'm not sure where Ezra fits into these stereotypes about autism, if he does at all. Or if any autistic kids really do. Ezra is not dependent on routine; he prefers the freedom to set his own agenda. His favorite type of play involves acting out and scripting scenes from books he loves or movies he watches. But, prescribed or not, he is most happy when bringing them to life, which is undoubtedly imaginative.

He doesn't fit other assumptions about autism, either. He is highly emotionally expressive. He connects emotionally with his eyes. We knew he was capable of spontaneous empathy when he came home to see Griffin crying and went to hug him. Rather than misunderstand other people's emotions, he is generally hyperaware of them. He works hard in his therapies, well aware of the different therapists' expectations of him. I worry, in fact, that he might be overly conscious of other people's expectations. Many times I've seen his confusion turn to distress when he didn't understand what someone wanted from him.

But then, there are ways in which he does fit the stereotype. He struggles so much with receptive and expressive language. When he does speak it's scripted, chunked, and not conversational. He rarely refers to us for information the way another kid might. He has those rigidities and anxieties about eating, and his odd relationship to music. He needs to be explicitly taught the expectations of each place he goes to. There are so few education options available in Massachusetts that I decide to call the Montessori school directly. I ask, "Would you be willing to have a child in your classroom who learns differently?" I brace myself for the answer. How many times have I weathered rejection of my son?

But she answers, "We would love to invite your son into our classroom."

The following week, Ezra and I go to visit the school. He brings his bucket full of animals (only farm animals now since *Charlotte's Web*, which he still watches obsessively), but he sets down the bucket when we enter the spacious, organized room. He runs around, excited. Everything is pale birch. Two ceiling fans spin above him. He runs from one to the other, thrilled, and points, something he doesn't always do.

"'Round and 'round!" he says.

He heads to one of the shelves and takes out a tray with wooden numbers and starts counting. The teacher, gentle and graceful, crouches beside him to show him how the lesson works. He listens briefly, but then he lifts the tray and goes to another table, a little trick he's learned ever since Griffin's started crawling, so he won't have to share.

"He likes to explore on his own," I say, defensive, and annoyed with myself for feeling defensive.

The teacher smiles at me. "Of course he does."

I breathe out. I like it here. I like the calm energy, this soft-spoken teacher. I like the idea that Ezra will have to learn to follow someone else's rules, something he hasn't quite mastered in the rest of his life. *Maybe,* I think, *this is where we can belong.*

On the drive home, I glimpse him in the rearview mirror. He sits with his bag of cheese puffs, looking out the window. He is so obtuse to me. My little boy, about whose thoughts I know almost nothing.

"Did you like it there, honey?" I ask, knowing he won't answer. "Would you like that to be your new school?"

I wish so much I could ever know what's in his mind.

I call Michael and tell him about the school. I tell him they're planning to hire a new assistant teacher, but as soon as they find one, in about a month, Ezra can start there. Then I hesitate. "Do you think he'll be okay with the fact that there are no toys?"

Michael asks what I mean, so I explain that all the items in the classroom are considered lessons. There are particular ways to use everything, and I can't imagine how that will go for Ezra, being told how he should play. Michael grows quiet.

"You don't think it's the right place for him?"

I hear it, that old defeat, the slipping, the falling, the blackness that threatens him whenever we talk about Ezra like this. He's

four years old

scared about Ezra, like I am. But we don't talk about it. No way. We can't go there. We can't risk the unfolding, the loss. We each have to be strong, seeing only progress and potential.

"I do," I say as cheerfully as I can. "I'm sure he'll do great there."

TODAY I AM wracked by grief. I hate it. I hate this grief. I hate its relentless grip, what it says about how I feel about my son. *What? What?* I want to say to it. I love Ezra as he is. I don't need him to be someone else. I don't want him to be someone else. So what is it, then? What *do* I want? I want . . . I want my son to be happy. I want him to be loved. I want that for me, too. Briefly, I let myself imagine it—Ezra without autism. It is silly. Impossible. His brain is his brain. But I imagine anyway. He is a completely different person, someone who has conversations and seeks out other children for play. I sit there. I make myself sit there. Am I happier? I try to pull away. I don't like this sort of thinking. I don't want to think this way about Ezra. But I make myself come back. I make myself look. Am I happier? I am . . . more comfortable. I don't worry as much about what he needs. I don't worry as much about how he will fare. I don't worry as much that he will be loved. With a swift cold shock, I realize my unhappiness is my own. It isn't his. It isn't his.

Still, this grief. It holds on to my sleeve today like a whiny child. Irrational. Pointless. *Go away, go away.*

Frank and I talk on the phone almost every day now. I shouldn't. I know that. But I'm unable to yank myself from this one thing that feels better than anything else in my life. We talk about art and writing and love. Writing this now, I hate myself. It's so obnoxious that I did this while love was right there in front of me, needing me to attend to it.

One day, while I'm supposed to be writing, while Ezra and Griffin are with Nadine, I browse clothes at the mall. This is my other vice (as if I need another); I use retail therapy. I have Frank on the phone. I tell him how just the other day I passed Michael in his car during his lunch hour. He didn't see me, his window was open, and he was smoking a cigarette.

"Can you believe it?" I said. "I had no idea he smoked! He's been hiding it from me."

"Guess you both have your secrets," Frank said.

About half an hour later, same phone call, I'm describing something, and in passing I say, " . . . because I love you." We both grow quiet. A woman reaches past me to look at a boot.

"Did you just say what I think you said?" Frank asks.

"No," I said.

"Yes, you did."

"I can't, though."

"But you did."

It just so happens that later that same day, Michael comes home from work pissed because our car broke down again, the one in which I had the accident, the one that the mechanics were supposed to have fixed.

four years old

"Don't let them charge us again," I say during our conversation about it, but I quickly realize I shouldn't have said this.

"I'm not an idiot," he roars. "Don't talk to me like I am."

He storms toward the stairs and throws my coat, which is sitting on the stairs, and my phone, which is inside, crashes against the wall. The bedroom door slams shut. I stand there, stunned. Griffin stands next to me, holding my leg. Ezra is downstairs, watching *Charlotte's Web*. He has just recovered, again, from a stomach flu. Nadine is out for the evening; I need not worry about her hearing. Griffin starts to cry. I scoop him up, furious, and walk to the top of the stairs. I open the bedroom door and say as calmly as I can, "Pack a bag and get out. I don't want you here."

I walk back to the kitchen, and soon I hear him come down and go out the front door. Griffin pats my chest, meaning he wants to nurse. I hold him close, not wanting him to absorb what's just happened. I feel surprisingly unafraid. I don't know what will happen next, but for now I just need to nurse Griffin, so I sit down to do so.

Ten minutes later, Michael walks back into the house. I don't dare look at him. I don't dare say a word. He stands in the doorway, the doorway to this house where neither of us really feels at home. I can feel his energy, tentative and scared.

"I'm sorry," he says. "You didn't deserve that. Please let me have another chance."

I look up at him. He's my husband. He's the father of my children. I know that I love him, even if I can't feel it at the moment.

"Okay," I tell him. "You get another chance."

That night we sit in the kitchen and discuss it.

"There hasn't been a break for me," he says. "This move we never should have done, the kids, Ezra's delays. I just need it all to slow down."

"But what if it doesn't?" I plead. "What if something else happens, and then something else? Even if our lives calm down, even when we come to the point where the kids are older and not so much work, new stuff will happen. Life is like that."

"I won't put myself in this position again," he says.

"In what position?" I ask. "With two kids? Married to me?"

He doesn't say anything.

"I need you to find a way to deal with it differently. I need you to stop blaming everything outside you for your unhappiness."

He runs a hand through his hair. Then he stands and pours himself a glass of water. He knows what I'm talking about. We've had this conversation so many times before. I've said to him so many times, "I want you to do what you need to take care of yourself. Exercise, take time for yourself, whatever you need." Still he doesn't. There's always an excuse: time, responsibility, et cetera, et cetera, et cetera. I'm so frustrated, so tired of it. And then I tell him about Frank. He listens, his expression unchanged.

He says, "I don't blame you. I would do the same in your position."

"So stop," I tell him. "I want us to be okay. I want to be with you."

four years old

He shakes his head, looks down into his water.

"I need to know you still love me, Michael," I say now. It is the only thing left I can think of. The only thing that can keep me here. Tears sting my eyes.

"I do still love you."

"I want to believe you," I say.

He comes over and hugs me, but he releases too soon.

Difficulty with Transitions

Michael and I don't do "date nights," those contrived stand-ins for romance that so many couples with new children have. I was never a fan of the date night. It seemed like maintenance sex, which strikes me as equally unappealing. But I start to see the allure. Maybe maintenance sex is better than no sex. Maybe date nights are better than divorce. There is a startling and disturbing statistic out there (although no one seems to know of its source) that 80 to 85 percent of couples with an autistic child wind up divorced. I don't like this statistic, and not just for the obvious reason of its suggestion that Michael and I are doomed. I am beginning to feel enraged that autism keeps being posed as this terrible monster that will destroy children, and now marriages as well. I want so much to believe that if my son's neurology is simply his neurology— meaning, if his brain makes him who he is, and he will always be autistic—then he can have a constructive effect on the world, on us. I know that he can, that he does. This is a mother's basic right, to know, to not have to argue, that her son is worthwhile. But statistics like this seem pitted against the possibility of my son's ever being accepted as a positive force.

But enough intellectualizing, enough thinking about such things. We arrange for Nadine to work a few hours one evening, and Michael and I go out to a local restaurant. All the eateries around here are fancy and overpriced, intended for rich vacationers. They give us one more reason to miss Portland. But we try not to talk about that tonight. We desperately need to enjoy ourselves. We sit at the bar and order glasses of wine and an entrée to share.

"I can't believe we're here by ourselves," I say.

"It's weird," Michael agrees.

Without the fog of feeding and diapering and playing with and keeping the children from harm, without the silent weight of our constant fears about Ezra, we are like different people.

Michael and I talk about the Montessori school. We laugh about Griffin, when he threw a balloon up over his head and said, "Wheee!" We look warmly at each other for the first time maybe in years.

More than a year before Ezra was born, Michael and I took a vacation to Baja, Mexico. We stayed at a resort where there were only two other couples. It felt like we were there all alone. The beach went on for miles with no one in sight, so we walked a ways and skinny-dipped in the turquoise water. We made love on the

four years old

sand, swam some more, and then we went back to our room for what has gone down in the history of our relationship as The Best Nap of Our Lives. Why the best? Because it was long and peaceful, lulled by the sounds and smells of the ocean, and because it was punctuated with more sex. Later, we had dinner in the resort's restaurant, where we were treated like royalty since we were the only ones dining. At that time, nothing bad had befallen us yet. We had not yet lost a pregnancy to miscarriage. We still had all the fantasies that come with being newlyweds: our future children, how our family would exude love.

We tried. I think we tried. But we couldn't have predicted how our shortcomings would get in the way. How Michael would blame me for our lives' not turning out like the fantasy promised. How, feeling that blame, I would reach to other things to feel better, such as new homes, new geography, a new man, which only harmed the marriage more. And I didn't know then what I know now: Michael and I stopped having sex because doing so makes us vulnerable together, and if we were vulnerable together we'd also be in our pain together, and to be in our pain together would mean to admit this one, difficult truth that we also *needed* to admit if we were going to be okay: that Ezra was autistic, that our fantasies about our lives together had taken a startling, unforeseen turn.

THE MONTH BEFORE Ezra starts at the Montessori school, Griffin turns one. Remember Griffin? Sweet little Griffin, with his soft wavy hair, with his big hazel eyes? His charming smile and funny little laugh? I haven't forgotten, I promise. But I'm frightened that with all the fuss about Ezra, Griffin will feel overlooked, less special. He has to come along for the therapies, work his day around Ezra's schedule. I worry that Ezra will say to me one day, when he finally has the words, "For Pete's sake! Stop analyzing every little thing I do!" (This, incidentally, is what every man in my life has said to me.) Meanwhile, Griffin will be out somewhere scoring crack, thinking we love his brother more than him.

On Griffin's birthday, we throw a party, and most of Michael's family and my father drive up. My mother flies in from Chicago. Our house fills with cousins and aunts and uncles, and Ezra watches with interest. This is progress, I think. No longer does he hide. No longer does he ignore everyone. He stays right in the middle of the chaos. Only once does he cry. I'm not right there when it happens. His cousin says Ezra didn't want him messing with his train tracks, but the bottom line is that we can rarely know or understand the reasons he might be upset.

In the evening, Ezra takes a bath, which is partially intended to help him poop. He is so often constipated, and baths, we've found, can help his muscles relax enough to have a bowel movement. When he's constipated, he appears more autistic. He goes inward, ignoring the world, trying to make himself feel better. The flipside of helping him to poop in the tub, of course, is that we wind up with poop in the bathwater, which, in case you were wondering, rarely retains a solid form after a few seconds. Michael has become an expert at helping Ezra out of the bath, bleaching the tub, and cleaning Ezra again in about five minutes flat. We chat with Michael's sister and her family while he performs the ritual, unfazed, as they look on with horror.

The next morning Ezra crawls into bed with his older cousin and snuggles (or "smuggles," as he calls it.) He's such a little lover this way. His cousins try to engage him. "Ezra," they say, "come look at this." "Ezra, do you want to play?" They are great kids, those cousins.

The day after the party, I pack a bag and drive with Griffin down to Connecticut to see Frank, whose wife is out of town. I am actually heading down there to go to IKEA, but since the store is in the same town where Frank lives, I know I will see him. What I don't understand is why Michael doesn't seem to care. He knows Frank lives in Connecticut. He knows because I can't mention his name without tacking on the phrase "from Connecticut."

Michael will ask me, "Who made you that CD?"

"My friend."

"Which friend?"

"Frank, from Connecticut."

He says, "Who was that on the phone?"

"My friend Frank."

"Got it."

"From Connecticut."

With all the distance between us, the arguments, the lack of sex or anything even resembling romance, does he really think I'm driving to Connecticut just to shop at IKEA? Still, he doesn't betray any concern. He does his wet-blanket shuffle around the house, like on any other weekend morning. He kisses Griffin (but not me), says goodbye, and that is that. Griffin falls asleep quickly in the car, and I drive in silence, trying not to think too hard about what I'm doing.

My hotel room in Connecticut is on the second floor. No one is around to help, so, with Griffin on my hip, I make three trips up the stairs to bring up my bag, the stroller (to sit Griffin in while he eats), and his portable crib. It hits me with some weight that this is what it would be like as a single mother. As soon as everything is inside, I call Frank. We make plans to have dinner in my room after my IKEA trip.

When he arrives later, I'm aware of how little I feel, how much my fantasy about what's between us is much more substantial than what is really between us. After dinner I change Griffin into his pajamas, give him nursies, and put him to sleep. Frank and I are alone. We blink at each other. Uh-oh.

We sit on the loveseat. I'm thankful it's in there, that the bed isn't the only choice for seating. We smile at each other.

"This is hard for me," he says.

I pull my legs up beneath me so I can face him. "What is?" I want to hear him say it.

"To be here alone, to not touch you, to feel so conflicted."

"You can touch me," I say. I stretch a leg toward him and he tentatively puts his hand on my shin. He smiles.

four years old

"I wish things could be different," he says.

"Me, too." I think of Michael at home with Ezra. It's nine o'clock at night, which means Ezra is watching *Charlotte's Web.* He's making Michael lie on the floor with him. It's how he keeps Michael with him, ensuring he isn't going to go anywhere. I look down at my little plastic cup of wine, feeling sad. "I can't think of things like that," I say. "Now that my kids are here, it's not possible for me to imagine another scenario."

"Of course." He begins to move his hand down my shin in little circles until he reaches the opening at my ankle, where he lets his fingers rest lightly. He doesn't really know what I mean. He doesn't have children. He doesn't have a kid with special needs. Our lives are so very different.

"If I weren't with Michael, would you want to be with me, really? With my two children? With Ezra?"

He doesn't answer at first. "I don't know. I've thought about it, obviously."

"I couldn't be with someone who didn't love my children completely."

"Of course you couldn't."

Sadness rushes through me again. I hadn't thought of it before, but who will be good enough if Michael and I don't work out? Who will love Ezra enough and entirely, just as he is? I don't want to wind up alone, but I will if I have to. I will if it means keeping my son safe.

Perhaps seeing my face, Frank says, "Let's talk about something else. Let's talk about when we first met."

"We were so free then." I smile.

"I was such an idiot," he says.

"That you were." His hand starts moving again, up under my pants, tracing the muscle in my calf.

"I should have chosen you."

"All these years," I say, "and here we still are."

He looks down at my leg, unhappily I think.

"I wish I knew better how to have what I want, how to be happy," he says after a bit.

I nod, knowing exactly what he means.

Later, after he leaves, after nothing more happens, I lie in bed, aware Griffin will soon be up, ready to nurse. I can set my nighttime clock by him. I wish Frank had kissed me. Just one kiss. Some days I think that's all I need. One romantic, loving, passionate kiss that will bring me back to life, back from this place where I spend too much time, where all I do is worry about Ezra and what is to come.

(Un)cooperative Play

Whenever we can, we try to see our friends who live an hour away. Before any of us had children, they visited us in Portland, and Michael and David bonded. They played some serious rounds

four years old

of Ping-Pong, drank beer, and made each other laugh. We were excited at the prospect of the men's seeing more of each other. Since Ezra was born, Michael's friends have dropped away. It's not their fault. It's his. He stopped calling people back. He stopped leaving the house. He stopped everything, retreating into some private space inside himself. I am so hopeful Michael will connect with David in a way that will help him emerge from that space.

We pack up some Frankenmilks and cheese puffs and snacks for Griffin. Ezra loves being in the car. He watches the world smudge past, thinking whatever he's thinking. We can't know. Griffin cries and fusses. He yells, "Eees!" which means he wants to nurse. He's always difficult in the car.

By the time we arrive, he's asleep. I carry him in his car seat while Michael helps Ezra, and his bucket of animals. Ezra walks in and goes straight for the girls' room. The older girl says, "Hi, Ezra!" and she follows him upstairs, where we know he will keep ignoring and moving away from her until she grows bored with him and comes back downstairs.

Michael and David are going to a bar to watch some baseball game, so they leave Kristin and me with the kids. I'm happy to do it, knowing Michael will have some time with David. I just want him to have some fun, some joy. I miss him. I miss the man I married, who seems long gone. Kristin makes us tea and she shares some concerns she has about her sister. Every five or so minutes I race upstairs to make sure Ezra is not smearing poop.

He isn't. Griffin wakes up and Kristin and I nurse our babies and then watch them toddle around together. Griffin falls on his tush and says, "Boom!" and we laugh. Ezra and her daughter come down and we put on a video for them and they watch together on the couch. There are these times, when things are normal and good, when I can almost believe my life is not so different from others'.

When we leave, Michael and David make a plan to watch the game regularly. They decide that every other Friday they will meet at a bar, alternately near us and near them. But they never follow through.

FRANK AND I keep talking on the phone. We are aware now of this word that has been uttered, which makes things between us feel weightier, like something is coming. And then something does come. He tells me he might be ready to leave his wife so we can be together. If only he had said this years ago, when I was single and wanted to be with him so badly I could feel it in my teeth. It's different now. I fantasize about being with Frank, but I want to be with Michael. I'm not ready to give up on us. Michael and I have children together, and they come first. If Michael and I didn't make it, whoever I was with next would have to love my children as his own. That person would have to love Griffin. He'd have to love and understand Ezra. Frank doesn't have kids. He wouldn't understand anything about my life the way it is.

four years old

I tell him I'm not ready and explain why. He is disappointed; he doesn't really have a choice.

Michael and I carry on, we diaper, we sleep, we dress, we feed. Then it is time for Ezra to start at the new school. We are hopeful. Oh, man, are we hopeful. It's ugly, the way we cling to everything that comes our way. We are so desperate, aching in our desire that our son will belong somewhere in the world.

I dress Ezra in his cutest clothes. He has so many cute clothes. I feed him cheese puffs and tell him we're going to school. I remind him of the fan and the little tray of numbers. He watches me skeptically, takes my hand and his bucket of animals, allows me to strap him into the car seat. The teacher is waiting for us when we arrive. I warned her about the bucket of animals, since the parent handbook asks that parents not let their children bring toys to school. She seems to understand Ezra will need an exception. She shows Ezra his cubby. She had asked me earlier which animal he likes, and she made him a polar bear symbol, which will be on all his stuff. But Ezra doesn't seem to care about the bear or understand what it all means. She shows him where to put his shoes. I bought him dinosaur slippers, especially for his time in the school. Already he starts to whimper a bit, frustrated that a stranger is talking at him, expecting things from him, needing him to understand. I put my hand on his shoulder and speak in my most gentle voice, and we point him toward the classroom.

I am to watch from an observation room. I appreciate this

allowance after the previous preschool, where I wasn't permitted to even watch. I duck into this space, my heart pounding. I watch him through the two-way mirror as he looks around the room and then heads straight for the math area, where there are red plastic triangular puzzle pieces that grow smaller and smaller in size, meant to explain multiplication. He pulls them out, one at a time, and drops them to the floor. I see the other children, who have been busy with their projects, who have been talking together like regular children do. I see them turn to look.

"Hey!" a little girl says. She's older than Ezra, dressed in a green dress over soft pants. She points at him. "You can't do that!" By now Ezra has dumped most of the lesson, tons of little red triangles of different sizes, on the floor. They skid under shelves and under the table, where the other children sit quietly, watching with interest. Anxiety weaves its way through my body. My little boy, my little boy. He doesn't understand. The older girl stands above him, hands on her hips. "Hey!" she says again.

The new assistant teacher goes to Ezra. My heart is in my throat. I feel already like I might cry. I watch as she crouches next to Ezra and tries to explain—explain!—that this behavior isn't allowed. (Has no one prepared her for Ezra's coming today?) He jumps a little, startled by her touch, and then a look of confusion comes across his face. That look, that terrible look that means, *I don't understand what this world needs from me.* He walks away, crying, leaving all those pieces on the floor.

four years old

I know I'm supposed to stay in that room, to allow them to figure things out by themselves, but that look . . . Sometimes I'm terrible
at this, at letting him be in the world with all his flaws, at trusting
other people to help him in the right ways, to accept him. So I come
out of the room and grab him. He looks at me, clearly surprised to
see me there. He thought I'd left. "Ezra," I say, aware of the children's
eyes, the teacher's eyes. "You can't just leave your mess on the ground.
You have to clean up. Come help me clean up." Then he screams.

I try to ignore this, as well as the stares, as I force him to pick
up the pieces. I put them back in their places, my face tight with
frustration, with grief. Ezra goes off to find something else to do,
and soon I go back into the room to watch what will happen next.

He finds letter boards. The purpose of these boards is to trace
your finger along the curve of the letter to gain a sensory experience
of the shape. I watched dubiously as a teacher showed another child.
The teacher took just two boards off the shelf and brought them to
the table, and then he slowly and meticulously showed the child as
he moved his own finger along the lines. I almost laughed. Ezra will
never stand for that. No way will he take just two random letters
from the shelf. He will need all of them. He needs always to have
all of whatever he's interested in. He will want to gather them into
his arms and then heave them to the table, where he will want no
one, especially not a stranger, determining what he has to do with
them. I put my head in my hands, rub at my eyes. Why did I ever
think this was going to work?

Sure enough, Ezra begins to pull the letter boards down from the shelf, one at a time, in order, so he can examine them from above. He's excited, arms flapping.

A little boy points in Ezra's direction. "Hey! You can't do that!"

The assistant teacher again comes to explain, and this time Ezra, looking more confused than before, cries and pushes her away. The teacher jumps back. In that brief moment I see her shadowy expression, a look that says, *This child is something to fear. This child is not normal.*

I open the door that leads from my little room.

"Ezra!" I call. I'm frightened for him, hurt, uncertain what else to do. He comes running into my arms. I hold him tightly, feeling his small, animal weight. I am sick with love for him. He wraps his arms around my neck and burrows his face into my shoulder. Like this, we go back to the car.

"It didn't go well," I tell Michael on the phone. By now, Ezra is fine. He is happy. He eats his cheese puffs, watching out the window.

"Oh no," Michael says. I can hear his despair, that downward slope. The responsibility I have here to keep him from going all the way down. "So that's it? It's over?"

"I don't know," I say.

That afternoon I receive an email from the head teacher: "Please let us try again. Lots of kids have a hard time the first few weeks. It's a big transition. But we really want Ezra to be a part of

four years old

our classroom. Two of the kids asked about him after he left. They said they'd like to see him again."

I take a deep breath, let it out slowly. Maybe I overreacted. Maybe I misinterpreted Ezra's reception. After years of feeling defensive and critiqued, after all the evaluations and other parents' comments, maybe I'm too quick to assume the worst. I thought the kids were judging him, but maybe they were just curious. Maybe he just needs to learn the rules, to grow confident.

"I'd like to try again," I wrote back. "But that assistant—she acted like Ezra was some kind of monster. He's not dangerous. He didn't understand why he couldn't play with everything the way he wanted to. That's all."

The head teacher promises she will talk to her.

The next morning, I buckle Ezra into his car seat.

"We're going to school," I say with as much excitement as I can muster. He begins to whimper. "It will be fun," I say. "And I'll be right there if you need me."

When we arrive, he takes my hand. He looks nervous to me. I'm sure I look nervous, too. But this is my job. I'm his mother. I'm supposed to nudge this small three-year-old into the world, even when it's scary. We take off his coat and shoes at his cubby and put on his dinosaur slippers. He goes with the teacher into the classroom, and I duck into the little observatory.

First, he tries to take a lesson from a small curly-haired girl. She looks up at him, surprised and upset to have her tranquility ruined. The other teachers aren't watching, so I run out to stop him. I know I shouldn't. I should just let his behavior unfold, let him figure it out. But I'm desperate right now; I'm too aware of how different from the other children he is, too aware of how much he needs, especially in this place. He starts to cry, so I direct him to another activity, fitting shapes into holes, and I disappear into the room again. His interest in this doesn't last long. He finds something else—a little pulley with a car—and when a teacher tries to show him how to use it, he throws it angrily to the floor. Next, he pulls down a book and begins to march around the room, making humming noises. I watch as the head teacher quietly tells another teacher to sit with him to read. She does, taking the book and pulling him gently by the hand. He goes along, confused, but is quiet as she opens the book and begins to read. I breathe out.

For the rest of the morning, every time he grows upset, this teacher takes him by the hand, finds a book, and reads to him. When it's time to leave, the head teacher says, "We have a way to calm him down now. We have books." She smiles in her gentle way while Ezra tugs at my hand to go. "That's a good start."

The third day of Montessori, Ezra starts to cry when we park in front of the school. He doesn't want to go, that much is clear. I don't know what to do. I'm a bad mother. I make him do things I shouldn't. I don't make him do enough. A week. I told myself we would give it a week. That seems fair.

four years old

I take Ezra by the hand and walk him inside. He's still crying. The nice teacher speaks gently to him about taking off his coat and shoes, putting them in the cubby. Ezra quiets down after a bit, still sniffling, but calmer. His expression is flat, worried. I don't want to see it, but I think he almost looks defeated. I can't think like that. I can't. I hand the teacher his Frankenmilk and bag of cheese puffs and go into the little room.

Ezra walks through the room, humming to himself. He finds the two items he knows he won't be scolded for. One is a tiny music box with a crank. The other is books. He moves between these two things over and over again. If another child comes along to see what he's doing, he picks up his item without looking up and moves away. This isn't right. I know this is no good. He's closing himself into a ball, trying to escape. He's making himself disappear.

Soon, Ezra begins trying to leave. He goes to the door and pulls it open. A teacher stops him. He cries.

"Home!" he calls out. "Home!"

What can I do? What else could I have done? I take him from the classroom, and we drive home.

In the car, I call Michael to tell him the news.

"Maybe he's just tired," he says. "Maybe he needs to eat more before he goes."

"No," I tell him. "No. We have to forget it."

Michael is silent. He feels just like I do, helpless, confused, and so very sad.

At home, Michael and I move through our evening motions. We diaper, we wash, we put the boys to bed.

I find him in front of CNN.

"I'm scared," I say. He turns, and when he sees my face, he comes to me. On the TV, a woman speaks urgently at the camera, something about war and two hundred lives and bombs.

"Don't be scared," Michael says. He's doing his part, taking his role.

"No," I say. "You need to be scared with me. You need to listen. There's no place for Ezra."

"Don't say that." A bomb explodes. The woman's voice speaks urgently in the background.

"How will he get through? How will we help him?"

I'm crying. Michael holds me close.

"Okay," he whispers. "Okay."

We say nothing else. Nothing else needs to be said. We hold each other. We know that we need each other.

Something breaks open then. I don't know what. It is the end of March. The world has begun to soften. Our child has autism. Somehow, we find, we have the strength to begin again.

* * *

Not Otherwise Specified

Something happens when Ezra reaches three and a half years old. His issues become more obvious. At three and a half, other kids start acting less strange, but not my own kid. I don't question as much anymore whether he is autistic, although there are certainly days he seems more autistic than others, and there are certainly days I still do question it. It's still possible to me that his difficulties with communication are unique, that they don't actually fit into a broad category, and that his communication issues are responsible for any trouble with social interaction. It is still possible that his behavior doesn't warrant the autism diagnosis, but I know this is the one he will have for the rest of his life.

I've heard of children in other parts of the country who sound very similar to Ezra, children with auditory processing issues and sensory processing disorders who never wind up on the spectrum. I've also heard of diagnoses given in other countries, like semantic processing disorder, which fits Ezra better than autism. And I can't help but wonder whether, if he didn't have such a severe speech and communication delay, autism would be the first place everyone went. Autism is such a huge spectrum, tremendous enough that I suspect in a few decades the medical community will be better at separating autism from other, more useful diagnoses. But for now, people see communication delay and they think autism. And once they think autism, there's no stopping them.

But I'm also less afraid to simply accept the label for now, even if it's not perfect. Ultimately, just as Ezra needs a language to communicate with us, just as he has to pour his thoughts into language that doesn't feel natural to him, we need a language with which to talk about him. It is unavoidable in the culture in which we live.

There is so much other language we've already had to take on: "problems with regulation," "problems with transitions," and "stimming." If Ezra were not a special-needs child, we could call these same responses tantrums, having too much fun to leave, and humming, all ways of talking about the exact same behavior, but in a positive way.

But he has not developed typically, and so much of what he does must be viewed through a negative lens. If he had developed the way everyone expected him to, he wouldn't be socially disordered; he'd be introverted, or someone who didn't need anyone's approval to enjoy himself. He wouldn't be slightly delayed in his gross motor skills; he'd be a kid who isn't that into sports. Even the word "autism," which comes from the Greek *autos*, means "self," as though being about one's self is a bad thing. Obviously, there is a line between functioning and not functioning, but no one seems to be monitoring where that line is and what it really means.

I take Ezra to an autism specialist, a kind, soft-spoken woman I immediately choose as our gal when she says on the phone, "I'm drawn to children with autism because I see so much of myself in

four years old

them. I have always struggled socially." She officially diagnoses him: pervasive developmental disorder, not otherwise specified. It means that he meets some, but not all, of the criteria for an autism diagnosis. It means he has atypical autism. It means "something's different, and we don't know exactly what." It means nothing, not really.

She also introduces us to relationship development intervention, or RDI. At first, like so much else, I feel enthusiastic about it. But over time, I lose my steam. RDI is a great concept. It's based on research that suggests that the autistic brain has the same connections as typical brains but the conveyance is slower. RDI practitioners believe that you can enhance those connections, make them smoother and faster, all by practicing various behaviors for a certain amount of time every day. The behaviors develop in children concepts such as togetherness, interdependence, and empathy. The therapy is based on having a relationship with your child and eliminating a lot of the regimented therapy that interferes with simply spending time with your child each day. Also, there is no "window of opportunity" in RDI. Any age can benefit.

For an approach that tries to remove schedules and stress from life, however, RDI is strictly controlled itself, and this is where I can't keep up. We are supposed to perform certain tasks every day at a certain time. Our family doesn't work this way. We don't do schedules or any sort of routine well. I could berate myself about this, of course, call myself lazy, uncommitted, a terrible mother once again. I'm awfully good at that. But I genuinely try RDI, and after just a few days, the therapy falls away and we go back to our loose lifestyle. Ultimately, we are who we are, and working against our natural ways of being never sticks.

EVERYONE KNOWS THAT having children transforms your life, but *how* they do that is personal, the beginning of a change that began long before the child was born. When Shannon the psychic said that Ezra was here to teach, she was doing one of her psychic tricks, like when your horoscope says, "Something good will happen this week." Well, of course it will, especially if you're looking for it. Of course Ezra is here to teach. All children are. The question I should have asked is "Will Michael and I be willing to learn?"

The same week that Michael and I decide to be more honest with each other, to admit our fears and desperation about our son, I receive an email from a friend in Portland whose son is also on the spectrum. A new school has opened, a school intended specifically for children on the spectrum. A school that celebrates its children and uses their interests to direct learning. The teachers, parents of autistic children themselves, have created a sensory immersion classroom. My friend's son, who hasn't been coping in a regular preschool classroom, is doing great there. He's trying new foods and learning to make friends. He calls it "the fun school."

Isn't it obvious what we need to do? We don't belong in Massachusetts. We can't make ourselves fit. Everything is harder when you don't belong. I'm trying so hard to change that for Ezra, trying

four years old

so hard to find him a home. Maybe we'll find a home for him in that new school in Portland. I lie in bed that night thinking it through, working out the logistics. If we do this, it will mean we will lose oodles of money: two cross-country moves; a house on the market at the start of a housing recession; the turmoil of relocating again.

The next morning I find Michael in the kitchen.

"Let's move back to Portland," I say.

He blinks. "Really?"

"Yes," I say. "Let's do it."

"Are you sure?"

"I'm absolutely sure."

His face brightens, and he comes over to hug me.

"Thank God! I hate it here."

I laugh. "Me too."

Like a miracle, Michael's old job takes him back, with a promotion. We ask our realtor to find us a house. That school has an opening for Ezra. Patty, his wonderful Portland speech therapist, fits him back into her schedule. We will lose Nadine because her visa is expiring, but I locate our original nanny. Turns out she's looking for a nanny position because she's about to return to school to be a nurse. Is it really possible that everything is working like this?

Before we leave Massachusetts, I work up the nerve to ask my father if he thinks he might be on the spectrum. At first he denies it. "I'm social," he says, which is a common misunderstanding about autism.

"Yes," I say. "But you don't really understand how to be social. You laugh along with me when I tell you you're being inappropriate, but in all these years you've never changed. It's finally occurring to me that you just might not get it."

I wait, wondering what he will say. He looks doubtful, but then again, in his mind, his social behavior is perfectly normal.

"You have no friends," I say. I'm not being mean. He says this about himself all the time. He thinks of it as an interesting fact. He actually has exactly one friend, Indian Joe, who isn't an Indian, but a blond guy with a ponytail who wears a cowboy hat every day of his life. Dad and Indian Joe see each other about once a year and talk about electronics and engineering, and pretty much nothing else.

"You're hyperlogical," I add.

He still looks dubious. "I'm not *hyper*logical," he says. "Everyone else is simply not logical enough."

"Do you ever feel like you don't understand something that everyone else in the world seems to?" I ask, trying another tactic.

Here, he thinks a moment. "There is something," he says then. "That thing that most people have, where they can imagine other people's feelings?"

"Empathy, Dad?"

"Yeah, empathy. I don't have any of that."

"You don't?"

"Nope."

I watch him, stunned. I've always felt loved by my father. He's a generous, caring man. But I've also always felt that he didn't consider my feelings. Or that he tried to, but couldn't. Now, here it is: a confession. Empathy. He doesn't have any.

"It's been a real problem in my relationships," he admits.

"I'll bet."

We both sit there a moment, nothing more to say.

I want to see Frank one last time, so we make a plan for him to drive up. That morning I shave my legs and blow-dry my hair. I put on my best underwear and bra. It's old habit, I guess. Nothing is going to happen. Nothing was ever going to happen, I realize now. I have to acknowledge that a small part of my desire to move to Portland is a wish to move away from Frank. Not that I don't love him. Not that I don't still feel like I might be in love with him. But my life has gone a different way, a way I couldn't have predicted.

About an hour before I expect him, he calls.

"I don't think I'm coming," he says.

Disappointment floods me, but, surprisingly, so does relief. "Why not?"

"We would just rake over the same coals all the reasons we can't be together."

I rub at a juice stain Griffin made on my pants.

"It was fun to see you when there was a chance something might happen. But now, knowing it won't, it will just be depressing."

"We're friends," I say. "Shouldn't friends want to see each

other?" I don't know why I'm pressuring him. I'm not sure I want to see him either, for similar reasons.

"Maybe after some time has passed," he says softly. "I'm not ready to just be friends."

I take in a breath. "I'm sorry."

"This has been a bad week for me," he says. "You kind of broke my heart."

"I'm sorry," I say again. I want to tell him my heart is broken, too, but it feels too intimate, and I need to direct any propensity for intimacy elsewhere right now.

"Yeah, well." I hear him breathing, maybe thinking through what he wants to say. "I feel like you were unfair with me. And don't say you're sorry again," he adds, when he hears me about to say I am. "You came close to me, you gave me hope, and then you yanked yourself away."

I bite my lip. "I wish I hadn't done that."

"But you did."

"My feelings for you were genuine. They *are* genuine."

He sighs. "If I didn't like you so goddamn much, I'd never talk to you again."

"I guess you're stuck with me."

"You're a terrible person," he says.

"I know you don't believe that."

"You're *something* not good."

"I'm screwed up. At least I can admit it."

When we hang up I feel sad, but also resolved. Frank and I

four years old

often discussed the idea that our relationship was pure fantasy. It seemed likely that if we were actually together, we wouldn't feel the same way. I can feel right now how true that is, how much we used each other to stay away from our feelings, our worlds. I did grow to care about him over time, but most of what we had wasn't real. I know that now. Meanwhile, I need to attend to my life. I need to stop trying to get away from it all the time.

We also have to say goodbye to Kristin and David. They drive up to spend the day with us, and we talk about how much this sucks. I can tell Kristin is doing her best to support us in whatever we need to do, but her disappointment is visible. We go to the kitchen to make a snack for the kids. I take out cheese and juice. She gathers cups.

"This move is about Ezra," I tell her. "You know that, right?"

She nods and looks seriously at me. "Of course I do."

But I know she doesn't really understand, not because she doesn't have a special-needs child, but because I hid my feelings about Ezra from her all this time.

"I know it must seem crazy to move so far, just to move back."

"You have a unique situation," she says. She unwraps cheese sticks and places them on a plate.

"Thanks," I say. I gather the cups to bring to the table. "I'm sorry it hasn't been what we hoped for." I don't know quite how to say this, or how to apologize for the space I've been in.

"Kerry," she says. "I don't even know what you're talking about. It's been so great. I'm just so sad you're leaving." Tears pop into her eyes.

"Oh, God," I say. "Stop! You can't cry!"

"It's all your fault!" she says, and this time the tears come for good.

We hug. I feel the same way, but I don't cry. I haven't cried in ages, I realize. I fear that if I let myself, I won't be able to stop them. A flood will come and I'll have to crawl into bed and won't be able to climb out. Tears are too dangerous right now.

"You'll notice I'm not crying," I say. "It's because I hate you."

She laughs. "I know," she says. "I hate you, too."

There will be a series of goodbyes. I have to shore up my reserves. Nadine will be leaving for Germany. We have to see our extended family one last time before we go. Also, we have to prepare for the six-day road trip across the country in our minivan, which sounds like the seventh circle of hell. At some point, I will cry. Long after we move back to Portland, I'll look back on this time and understand that this was the year that my whole life dropped open, unraveled. I will never again be able to grip those fantasies about what I thought my life would be—my marriage, my children, my sense of myself as a mother. I will never again be able to trust that the world is unquestionably safe and welcoming to my son. I will always be vigilant.

But for now, I'm heading to Portland, where we started. If I have a home at all, it must be this place where we began, where my children began, where our hopes began. We have to go back to our origins sometimes to find out where we wound up.

four years old

Summer in Oregon

SEVEN YEARS OLD

Parallel Play

On a sunny morning in the very beginning of June, we leave Massachusetts. There is a thought that sits at the edge of my consciousness—we move and move and move, and still we are just us. We have tried to move away from our sorrow about our son—not our son, but the loss of the expectations we had about what our lives might be with our son. Yes, of course. Everyone knows that geographical cures don't exist. But we all need to feel like we have a home, and this is the truest reason for our going back to Portland.

From the back seat, Ezra says, "Draw a kangaroo?"

I look back at him. "You want me to draw a kangaroo?"

"Okay."

Michael and I both have this habit with Ezra, repeating what he asks, making sure we've got it right.

I look at Michael for help, but he just smiles. "I have no idea how to draw a kangaroo," he says. He's feeling smug because usually he's the one Ezra asks to draw something, and there are few things Michael hates more than arts and crafts. It's something Ezra has been way into these past few months. He asks us to draw various characters from his favorite DVDs, and then he wants us to cut them out so he can use them to reenact scenes he remembers. It's cute, but it leads to hundreds of little pieces of paper scattered all over the house and the car.

I pull out a pad of paper and pen and try to remember what those kangaroos at the zoo looked like.

"Do their ears stand up or hang down?" I ask Michael.

"Up," he says.

"Draw a kangaroo?"

"I'm working on it," I say, and then to Michael, "He thinks we're all Picasso."

"Ah, but we are," Michael says. "You usually can't tell what Picasso's subjects were either."

"Draw a kangaroo?"

I sketch something quickly that looks more like a dog with deformed front legs than a kangaroo, and I hand it back to Ezra.

"Here you go," I say.

He looks at it a moment with disapproval and drops it to the floor.

"Draw a caterpillar?"

seven years old

A caterpillar, I can do. I make one for him and give it to him. This he stares at, clearly pleased. Then he hands it back to me.

"Cut the caterpillar?"

Of course. I carefully rip it out. When I give it back to him he makes it do a little dance, and then he adds it to the six or seven other torn pieces of paper that he's tucked into the seat beside him.

If Ezra could have his way, I think he would prefer we all just stay in the car for the whole trip. He likes this, Mommy and Daddy and even Griffin, whom he could usually take or leave, all in sight, strapped together into our moving machine. He likes the soft rumbling beneath him and the flashing world outside the window. He likes being able to watch *Wonder Pets* over and over, quickly coming to know every song so he can sing along. The first time we pull into a rest area to pee, Ezra screams as soon as Michael steps out.

"Daddy back in car-a?" he says between sobs.

So from then on—for the next three thousand miles—Michael pees into bottles.

"Don't look," he says when he feels my eyes on him.

I start to giggle.

"And don't laugh. I can't do it if you're looking or laughing."

I turn my head, doing my best to suppress my laughter. When I hear the stream hit the bottle, though, I can't help myself. I glance over, in hysterics. "Are you going to fill that bottle?"

"Probably."

"This is too ridiculous," I say.

He finishes, shakes, and then opens the door to dump the pee. "Gross," Michael says, giggling now as he watches his urine splash on the cement.

Ezra says, "Close it," referring to the door.

Griffin is less enthused by being in the car. He, like Ezra, appreciates having his family close by, but he'd much rather have them even closer, like in one another's arms. He also is bored with the same DVD and toys all the time.

But the hotel, oh, the glorious hotel! The kids come running into the room with smiles on their faces. Griffin finds the remote control, his favorite of all toys, and starts pushing buttons. Ezra picks up the receiver of the telephone.

"Hello," he says. "Hello, Mommy."

They love hotels. Who doesn't, really? Those little soaps, HBO, three towels after your shower, if you so please. You can make as big a mess as you want and you don't have to clean it up. You can watch a *My Fair Brady* marathon and know doing so says nothing about you because it's just this one time, because you're in a hotel where real life is suspended. This room is on the main floor and has sliding glass doors to the parking lot, so Ezra can keep track of Daddy as he unloads the car. And keep track he does. He stands by those doors, watching intently, until Michael is done.

Griffin has a new word: "no." He says it "bo," like the name of the guy from *The Dukes of Hazzard*. Ezra says, "Mo?" Both of them say no as a question, an inflection that makes it sound like, "Are you

seven years old

stupid?" But while Ezra's is a quick "mo?" Griffin draws his out so it sounds like "bo-o-o-o?"

This new word is incredibly useful. It means we can readily know what Griffin doesn't want, which is a revelation for the parents of our almost four-year-old Ezra, who only about six months ago started answering okay or "mo?" and not consistently. We ask Griffin hundreds of questions, charmed by his ability to answer.

"Griffin, do you want this cracker?"

"Bo-o-o-o?"

"Do you want to take a nappy?"

"Bo-o-o-o?"

"Do you want to go with Daddy?"

"Bo-o-o-o?"

"What about nursies? Do you want some nursies?"

Griffin smiles, revealing the gap between his two front teeth. We call it his David Letterman smile. He's onto the game. He knows we like to hear him say, "Bo-o-o-o?" but he can't say, "Bo-o-o-o" to nursies. He doesn't have it in him.

"Eees," he finally affirms, that crazy smile still on his face.

FOR SOME REASON, the DVD player in the car keeps opening and restarting from the beginning. Amazingly, Ezra doesn't seem too upset by it. For him it means another chance to watch *Wonder Pets* without having to ask for it. Michael and I spend some time trying to figure out the reason for it, however, because even if Ezra and

Griffin don't care, it's making us crazy. If I have to hear the *Wonder Pets* blowfish song one more time, I might strangle someone. First, we assume the DVD player is affected by bumps in the road, but it doesn't seem to correlate with any bumps. Then we consider that the wire connecting the machine to its power lies alongside Michael, and every time he moves, it affects the power. But when I sit in the back seat to nurse Griffin, I see OPEN displayed on the screen, which supposedly means that the actual DVD eject button has been pushed. We don't think Ezra can reach it to do that himself, so it remains a very annoying mystery.

Every time it starts over, Ezra counts to himself to remain calm. He counts his fingers.

"Let's count fingers!" he says. "One, two, three, four, five."

He counts over and over again until the DVD is replaying.

Today is one of those days when Ezra acts so normal that I question whether he's really so different. He drops his cup on the floor when he finishes his milk, and when I say, scolding, "Ezra!" he shocks us all by replying, "Sorry." The next time, he hands it back to me and says, "All done."

I say, "Ezra, look at the choo-choo train," and he looks out the window and points.

"Chugga chugga chugga chugga choo-choo!" he sings.

We play I Spy with My Little Eye. Outside the window are long flat fields of wheat and corn. I can see what's coming for miles. Black birds with red breasts settle onto fence posts and an occasional tree.

seven years old

"I spy with my little eye something that's white and fluffy and up in the sky," I say. "What is it?"

"De de," Griffin says nonsensically, always wanting to be the first to answer.

"Clouds," Ezra says.

"That's right!"

"I spy with my little eye something that's black and red and says *tweet tweet*. What is it?"

"De de."

"Birdie," Ezra says.

"Right! Now it's your turn."

"I spy with my little eye something that's yellow water," Ezra says. It's what he always says, although only Michael and I, who are used to Ezra-ese, would understand it.

"Yellow water is pee-pee," Michael says, which is what we always say back. And Ezra laughs, seeing our smiling faces, his joke never losing its humor.

Griffin holds a cookie box that has little pictures on it. He digs his little chubby hand in there and pulls out the cookies one at a time while he watches whatever DVD is playing. He's wearing only a diaper and a T-shirt that's covered with stains from the strawberries he ate earlier. The shirt rides up, exposing his fat belly. Griffin's cookie box catches Ezra's eye.

"Want box?" he says, reaching for it.

I lean back and pull the bag of cookies out for Griffin and

hand Ezra the box. Griffin doesn't even flinch. Ezra examines the pictures on the box a moment and then hands it to me.

"Cut the sun?" he says. On the box is a tiny picture of a sun. I know it will soon wind up on the floor with the many other pictures. It's so small. I doubt he'll keep track of it for more than a few minutes. But if he wants me to cut out that sun for him, I'll do it. I'd do most anything for him.

We had originally planned to stop at zoos and children's museums as we drove cross-country, but at our first stop both boys had meltdowns at the Binghamton Zoo, which was under construction, and so we decided to stick to playgrounds instead.

At one of the playgrounds, Ezra climbs the wooden structure and tentatively approaches the slide. He is overly cautious like this with most everything, always afraid he might have a feeling or sensation for which he didn't prepare. While other kids jump from high platforms and race around on tricycles, Ezra won't even go down the slide alone. This is a part of what the occupational therapists have labeled "problems with self-regulation." He doesn't feel confident handling the unfamiliar.

"Catch it," he says to me—a line from *Wonder Pets*—but I know what he means: *Catch me.* I hold him lightly under his arms and help him go slowly down the slide.

A boy around four or five years old, a year or so older than Ezra, approaches him.

"I'm going to go down that slide, too!" he tells Ezra. His mother

seven years old

smiles at me. I can feel the tension inside me rise. It seems I brace myself for almost every interaction.

"Cheese, cabbage, popcorn," Ezra says to the boy, quoting again from one of his DVDs. This is what he usually says to kids who are older than he is, I think because in one particular DVD the girl who reads these words from a book is older than Ezra. But it's hard to know why. He smiles as he says it. At times like this, I feel glad his speech is so unintelligible. The boy just smiles back and races around to the ladder for the slide.

"How old is he?" the mother asks. I look for evidence that she's wondering what's wrong with him, but I don't see any in her expression. Ezra is small for his age, so most people still see him as a baby, which is always a relief.

"He's three," I say. It isn't really a lie. He's closer to four than three, but officially he *is* still three. I analyze her reaction, but it is just a pleasant smile.

"Cute," she says, and I release my breath.

Today, Ezra's autism seems to be the biggest thing about him. He flaps his arms with excitement. When he hits his toe on a toy, he says a line from *Wonder Pets*: "Are you okay, Ming Ming?" When he drips the tiniest bit of Frankenmilk on his shirt he screams, "Shirt off!" He ignores every last question we ask him, and then finally smiles and says, "PBS kids," as though this is a meaningful answer.

At the playground, rather than go down the slide or run around like the other children, he brings out his crayons and pad of paper. "Draw Moose A. Moose?" he tells me. The fictional animated character Moose A. Moose is his new obsession, replacing *Wonder Pets*. We bought a DVD starring Moose A. Moose online. We pulled it out yesterday, knowing he would love it, and now this is all he wants to watch. In a matter of twenty-four hours, I've learned to draw a pretty impressive Moose A. Moose, so I do.

"Blue Zee? Draw a blue Zee?" Zee D. Bird is Moose A. Moose's best friend. "Moose A. Moose's green shirt?" I make a green T-shirt for Moose A. Moose.

"Moose A. Moose's green hat?" I make the hat.

"Zee's green shirt? Green hat?" I color these, too.

"Moose A. Moose's black shirt?" And so it goes, until we have dressed Moose A. Moose and Zee in all the many different outfits they wear in the DVDs. Then we come to the next phase.

"Cut Moose A. Moose?"

By the time we are done, a good half hour later, Ezra has every ripped-out paper version of Moose A. Moose and Zee he has seen on DVD. He analyzes them carefully, making sure he has all the colored shirts and hats he needs.

"Zee's harmomica?" he says, with a double *m*.

"Zee's harmonica?" I ask, making sure I've got it right.

"Zee's harmomica?" he confirms.

I sketch out the best harmonica I can, rip it out, and put it up to my lips.

seven years old

"Wa-wa-wa-wa," I sing, pretending to play it. Ezra likes this. He puts it to his lips.

"Wa-wa-wa-wa," he says. We smile at each other.

Next, he focuses on scripting the scenes. I watch him, wishing I could understand better what he says. Wishing I could understand better *why* he says what he says. Later, Ezra gathers up all the pieces of paper and stuffs them beside him in his car seat.

"Moose A. Moose?" he says.

"You want to watch Moose A. Moose?" Michael asks.

Ezra says nothing. He watches his leg as it kicks the back of my seat.

"Ezra," Michael says, more forcefully. "Do you want to watch Moose A. Moose?"

Ezra looks out the window now, still silent.

"Ezra!" Michael yells, but still nothing.

"Ezra," I say in a soft voice. "Answer Daddy." I put my hand on his leg, trying to capture his attention. Michael and I know full well he wants to watch the DVD, but we want him to communicate with us, to answer our questions. We are so scared when he does this, when he disappears. But he doesn't look at me. Finally, because we have to go, because we have to move forward, because we can't sit here all day trying to lure our son to come back to us, we put on the DVD for him.

From the car we see rows and rows of windmills. They are giant fans spaced evenly and perfectly like soldiers through the landscape. They each have three white blades that on this blustery day flip quickly and then slow down, none of them following the exact same pattern.

"Ezra!" I say, excited for him. "Look at all the windmills!"

I watch as he looks out the window and recognition comes over his face. He smiles and his whole body jerks with pleasure. "Windmills!" he says, imitating the word.

"So many of them," I add.

He points. "'Round and 'round!"

"Yes, they're going around and around."

"One, two, three, four, five windmills!"

"Yes, lots and lots of windmills."

He twists around to watch as we hurtle past them, all that lovely, organized movement—all that repetition and pattern, again and again and again and again.

In the next town, we pull off the highway to fill up and find something to eat. There is almost nothing here, just long stretches of landscape with mountains in the distance. I don't know how people live here, how they sit inside the endless stretch of their own lives.

We stop in a restaurant parking lot, and as soon as we open the car doors, Ezra starts crying.

"You've got to be kidding, Ezra," I say to him. "We've been driving for hours! How could you not want out of this car?"

He doesn't answer, of course, but keeps crying. I unbuckle him and haul him onto the pavement.

seven years old

"Great," Michael says. "How is this going to work?"

"Maybe there will be something inside to distract him." We look at each other and know better. "Then I'll go inside and order us something," I say.

"What am I supposed to do with the boys?" he asks.

"You stay out here with Ezra and I'll bring Griffin inside with me."

Michael sighs, resigned. I take Griffin and head inside. I let him run back and forth in the entryway for a bit. He presses his sticky little hands on the glass and then crashes himself into the ugly brown couch again and again. I scan the menu and order as quickly as I can. Inside the restaurant, I glimpse a family like mine, but nothing like mine. They sit at a table, eating and talking. People tell me all the time that children eventually grow up, that even the things that are hard to imagine do come to pass.

With Ezra, though, that growing up is so uncertain. There is nothing that tells us he will ever communicate easily or stop crying when someone sings "Twinkle, Twinkle, Little Star." True, he has dropped tons of behaviors we worried he'd never lose. He's grown comfortable with other kids and surprising noises. There was a time we worried he'd never talk, and now he does. There are plenty of skills, too, that we don't know he has and then, all of a sudden, we see him doing them. When it comes to Ezra, we can't look to timelines—as most parents can—and know basically when to expect something. We can't assume that anything we do or make him do, like all the therapies, will ever affect his development. As with most children on the spectrum, his development follows its own unwritten path. Skills will come, others won't, and then they'll disappear and come back. His development is like a magic show. Again and again I have to remind myself to stop trying to control it.

Back outside, Ezra is strapped into his car seat, Moose A. Moose on the portable DVD. Michael is in the driver's seat, his eyes closed, head back.

"What the hell?" My voice startles him.

"He wouldn't stop crying, so I finally gave him what he wanted."

I shake my head and put Griffin back into his seat, although I'm sure I would have done the same thing.

WE CROSS THE state line into Oregon three days later, haggard, exhausted, and relieved. We ride through the familiar landscape, the heavy green spectrum of northwestern firs and maples and oaks. We stop at a campground in the Columbia Gorge, which is one of the most beautiful places I've ever spent time. Gray craggy rocks and old purple lava flows, green mountains and the shocking blue of the Columbia River. Windsurfers dot the river like thumbtacks in a map.

Michael and I, separately before we met and then together, spent many afternoons in our twenties hiking through these forests, breathing the oxygen-filled damp air. We were married out here. We both have many memories of camping beneath a thick blanket

seven years old

of stars and laughing with friends as we sat around a sparking camp-fire. Many of those memories are laden with difficult feelings that I struggled with at the time, mostly feelings about boys.

It's hard to believe I ever thought anything was hard before hav-ing to navigate the world as a parent, and especially of a child with disabilities. I spent so much of my twenties wishing I could find the right guy, wanting a life that included marriage and kids. I never considered what that life would actually be when it arrived. There are times I'm furious with myself about that, about my inability to just sit inside my life. I pushed and pushed to have a baby, but I never allowed room for genuine contentment with my marriage. It's my fault that Michael and I are where we are. It's my fault that whatever we had was never the right thing, or enough. We had babies, we moved, we lost money again and again. That's my fault. No wonder Michael gave up eventually on trying to make me happy. No wonder he just gave in to the depression, to the helplessness.

We walk up the hill, past ferns and ancient firs, and the boys skip along ahead of us. A car slowly drives through and we grab their hands, pulling them to the side.

"Hi!" Griffin calls to the people in the car. His speech has blos-somed. He suddenly has tons of words.

"Hi!" they say back, grinning.

It's so different having a child like this, a child who eas-ily delights people, giving them what they want. It helps me see how much people need this. No one likes to feel that someone isn't interested in them, that they could go unnoticed. As much as people love the way Griffin responds to them now, I worry some about his future. I'm concerned that he'll be too caught up in wanting people's acknowledgment. I expect I'll have to hold his hand through much heartbreak. Already I can feel the strain in my heart for him, can picture the nights I'll cry in my pillow after I've helped him through some terrible hurt. The list just goes on and on, doesn't it? An endless field of reasons to feel scared for my children, for myself, special needs or not. I often think I'm not cut out for parenting, but it's sort of too late for that kind of thinking.

I stop to peer at a small purple flower. I don't know its name, but I don't need to. It has wild spidery petals, its pollen center hidden inside. Two purple fanglike petals point toward its stem.

"Ezra," I say. "Come see this flower!"

Amazingly, he comes over to peer at it. I never know when he's going to enter my world like this, and so willingly, without my having to work at it. I watch his face as he smiles. I don't know what's in his mind, if he sees the flower's unique loveliness the same way I do.

"Purple flower," he says and points to touch it.

"Yes," I say. "Pretty purple flower."

He stares at it a moment.

"Moose A. Moose's flower?" he asks.

"Sure," I say. "It's Moose A. Moose's flower." Who knows what happens in that brain of his?

seven years old

After diaper changes and runs to the bathroom, we climb back into the car. When Michael turns on the ignition, Moose A. Moose starts playing on the DVD. The boys stare wide-eyed, as though they've never seen the movie before, as though this isn't the fifty-seventh time they've watched Moose A. Moose do his dance about spring's arrival.

Michael looks over at me, seeing my irritation.

"We're almost there," he says.

I nod. "Then it's merely eighteen or so more years and we should be done." I'm aware immediately after I say this that it may well be more than eighteen years of parenting Ezra. I hold my breath, afraid I've upset Michael.

But he simply says, "We'll wish they were little again."

I laugh. "Hard to grasp it."

"Yet that's the way it is," he says.

I look back at them, at their sweet chubby faces, their beautiful bright eyes. I could eat those kids, they're so delicious.

And then, finally, Portland. Michael and I exclaim as we drive through the neighborhoods. The old Craftsman-style homes, the bungalows, the native gardens. It is all so familiar to us, so homey. How could we ever have left?

During our first week back, we take a drive to the old neighborhood. We ride slowly up the slight hill of our old street. Dread washes through me as we approach the old house. Of course, there is nothing to dread anymore. That time—when we worried and stood terrified before our son, wondering what would come—that time is over. Not that we won't still worry. We will. We do. But the quality of concern is different. I don't think as much about amorphous concepts like "independence" or "institutions." I can see now that Ezra is like any other almost four-year-old in most ways. His struggles with communication are severe, but he continues to progress. The promise that progress offers is immeasurable for me.

"Do you think he remembers living here?" Michael asks as we drive by the house. The new owners have kept up the garden in the front. They've repaired the peeling paint on the siding. It looks nice. I glance back at Ezra, who is looking down at a book. He's not concerned with what's outside the window.

"I have no idea," I say. First memories of my own childhood home come to mind. The interior of the house we moved out of before I turned two. I can see it, its shadows, the odd sense of its unintelligibility. I remember a dream: I lie in my parents' bed with only my mother. My father isn't there. A window up high, as though I'm looking at it from the basement. A fox stops to nibble at greenery there.

I ask my mother, "Is it morning yet?"

"Not yet," she tells me. "Not yet. Go back to sleep."

Maybe it wasn't a dream. Maybe it was only partially a dream.

In another house, I remember feeling scared all the time of nightmares. I cry and cry because I don't want to sleep, because I don't want to wake again inside the strange shadows of my room.

seven years old

What memories have we already built for Ezra? What will he remember? I can't know, and of course he can't tell me. He stares at the pages of his book, deep in his own thoughts. This remains shocking for me each time I come up against it: how unknowable our children are, how separate we all must be.

Augmentative Communication

Ezra goes back to Patti for speech therapy. He starts at the new school, which is warm and homelike. The first day we bring him there, I watch as they approach Ezra. They don't overwhelm him. They let him explore on his own. They tell us that the most important thing they work on is their relationship with each child, that this is always the gateway to helping them. When I pick him up in the afternoons, he is happy, jumping back and forth through the room, arms flapping. They tell me how well he is doing, how intelligent he is, how much they enjoy having him around.

In the car, I ask him, "Did you have fun at school today, Ezra?"

He doesn't answer, of course. But it doesn't matter. I trust he did. And for that I feel so grateful.

At home, Ezra rushes into the house, something urgent on his mind.

"Moose A. Moose black shirt?" he says to me.

I start toward the paper and crayons, but he stops me.

"Mo?" he argues, still using his word for "no." He takes my hand and pulls me to his dresser. "Black shirt?"

I open the drawer to find him a black shirt, wondering what he's up to. When I find one, he gestures for me to put it over his head.

"Black pants?"

Ah, I see where this is going. I gather up the black pants, black shoes, and a black hat, and I help him put on the full ensemble. He marches around the new living room in the outfit and sings while Griffin laughs and chases him, calling out his own special moniker for Ezra: "Dezwa! Dezwa!"

Then Ezra comes back to the dresser. "Moose A. Moose green shirt?" he says. And so it goes, until he has worn Moose A. Moose's costume for every DVD that exists.

As Griffin's speech develops, he talks incessantly about Ezra. If I ask him what he's doing, he tells me what Ezra is doing. If I ask him what he wants, he answers, but then goes to Ezra, "Dezwa, ee want some?" Even though our house is relatively small, if Ezra walks out of the room, which he often does, in search of something more interesting than us, Griffin says, "Let's go see Dezwa." Again and again, he makes me stand up from where I've been sitting comfortably so that we can follow Ezra. I eventually snap at him, "Griffin, if you want to go where Ezra is, then go! Why do I have to come?"

Griffin's development is so different from Ezra's, and yet it orbits around Ezra. Everything Griffin does hinges lovingly, admiringly on his brother.

Sometimes, Griffin's development brings up—again—that grief, that pointless, foolish grief: Our lives will never be like other people's, all those expectations and hopes for my son severed. I hate it. I hate that it still can take hold of me, no matter how I shoo it away, no matter how meaningless it is. This grief comes unexpectedly, without purpose, and often it comes just as sharply as the first time it did, when I first understood my older child would be different from typical children. The stages of grief—this idea that people will pass through necessary levels, and then be done—are a ridiculous myth. Like so much else we cling to, the notion that people can be fit into boxes, that we all progress through life the same way, is a bunch of hooey. Grief is solid and slippery—an eel that moves through the body, resurfacing here and there.

Griffin also has behaviors typical of autistics: He flips over toy cars and spins their wheels. He flaps his arms when he's excited. He makes a repetitive noise and runs in circles. Michael and I joke to each other when he acts like this, "Uh-oh, Griffin just became autistic. Oh no, wait. He's cured!"

Watching Griffin grow has been enlightening for Michael and me. We can see how different Griffin and Ezra are—not just in their acquisition of language, but in how they interact with the world. From around eight or nine months, Griffin has been unlike Ezra in essential ways. Griffin references us constantly, while Ezra, although he did some social referencing, did so way less. Griffin derives pleasure from responding to us in a way Ezra never has.

Where Ezra can be deeply fascinated by books or the pattern of sunlight through the trees, Griffin wants only people. Ezra connects differently with people, with the world, than another child might, than a child like Griffin does.

It is more obvious than ever that Griffin thinks like Michael and me, whereas Ezra thinks another way. With Griffin here, I finally understand why I always felt unusual as a parent. Why it always seemed more difficult, or more extraordinary, to parent Ezra. With Griffin, I just talk to him. I do what I do everywhere in my life to connect, to be understood. With Ezra, I've had to be more creative. I've had to stretch beyond my normal range of behavior. I've had to push myself, to question myself. I've had to sit with the fact that I can't know what he's thinking most of the time, that I can't know much about his needs or the way he sees the world. When Michael and Griffin and I see a rainbow, I believe we all see the same thing. When Ezra sees that rainbow, it might be something else to him. The infamous high-functioning autistic woman Temple Grandin explains, in her book *Thinking in Pictures,* how she thinks about things as images, not words. If you say "horse," for example, a slideshow of the five horses Grandin knows begins to play in her mind. Perhaps it's the same for my son. I just can't know.

RIGHT AROUND EZRA'S fourth birthday, some very good things happen: He potty-trains in just one day. He learns to use the computer mouse at the school, which means he can engage visually with the world in a way that thrills him and us. It means he can feel connected. He shows us on the computer how much he understands. When we say, "Find the circle and put it in the square," he rarely responds. But when Elmo says it online, he immediately moves the mouse over the circle and drops it in the square. He processes the words and directions of the visual world quickly, with no lag time, no repeating, and no slowing down in the ways that he requires when the world is solely aural.

Also, an assistant at Ezra's new school tells us that rice milk constipates her own son, so we switch to straight milk cut with water and, like magic, he is no longer stopped up.

Not all the changes are good, though. He also suddenly starts to hit when he is upset. He hits only Michael, his nanny, and me, and only when we tell him he isn't allowed to do something. We hold his arms down and take him to his room to calm down. We say, "No hitting." We're a bit at a loss, because Ezra's never been a discipline problem. We rummage through his supplements, trying to figure out what's changed. We comb through his days, worried something's gone wrong. After a few days it also occurs to me that he's just a four-year-old, with new emotions and new skills, like the potty training. We endlessly play this game: *Is it autism or is it normal?* I am tired of trying to ride this line between helping him and hovering, of possibly creating something that isn't even there. I fear Ezra is tired of it, too. In a few years, when Griffin turns four, he will have trouble with hitting as well, enough so that he'll need a positive-reinforcement chart at his school so he'll stop expressing his frustration with his hands.

Once, with Griffin down for his nap and Ezra playing quietly, I check my email. I become engrossed in a friend's story, a friend I haven't spoken with in years. I write her back, eager for the adult connection that is so often missing from a parent's life with young children. I click "send" and am suddenly uneasy. Where is Ezra? The back door is wide open. I didn't hear it. He is always so quiet, so stealthy, so unconcerned with what his father and I know. My heart picks up its pace and I run outside. "Ezra?" I call. "Ezra?" He's not in the yard. I stupidly left the gate open when we last came inside. Stupid! How could I do that? My chest grows tight, and I run down the block, calling for him. What will he do if he is lost? He can't answer a stranger's questions. He can't tell them where he lives. He could never ward off a kidnapper or molester or . . . I can't think like this.

"Ezra!" I run back to the house, tears at my eyes. Maybe he came inside again. I run through the rooms, but he's not there, he's not there. My limbs feel jellylike, numb. I race back outside, a new thought. *Please,* I think. *Please.* There is a hole in the shrubbery between our yard and the neighbor's. *Please.* I climb through, and my God! There he is. His small, small body. His blond mop. He turns to see me and smiles, unaware of the panic, unaware of the world as anything other than soft and forgiving.

I grab him by the arm, enraged, desperately thankful, sick.

seven years old

"Don't ever go through there again, Ezra. Do you hear me? Don't you ever leave this yard by yourself."

I know my words mean nothing. I know he doesn't understand me. Or, rather, I don't ever know what he understands. I lock the door, close the gate. We buy chicken wire and fence in that hole on the weekend.

On another day, we have a friend and her child over. Griffin and the kid toddle off together to play in his room while she and I talk. A car alarm goes off—*beep, beep, beep*—repetitive and rhythmic.

"I wish someone would turn their car alarm off," I say.

"No shit," my friend says.

Then it occurs to me. Jesus Christ. I run outside and sure enough, there is Ezra, in my car, honking the horn in perfect rhythm. He smiles at me, pleased with himself. I pull him out of the car while he resists.

"No, Ezra! No! You don't ever go outside without an adult!"

ALTHOUGH FEARS AND frustration regularly trigger me, I must admit to myself that Ezra has progressed in nearly every area of his life. Except eating. He is growing and learning and is even potty trained. He's involved with the world in a larger way now, which leads him to think about what else might be out there, beyond the confines of our yard. But the eating issue has not budged. Not even a little bit. I've offered him macaroni and cheese, plain noodles, cereal, cream of wheat with milk, chocolate milk, goldfish crackers, animal crackers, pizza, carrots, apples, bananas, string beans, candy, peanut butter, juice.

"No, thank," he says each time, pushing my hand away, turning his head.

Friends ask, "Have you tried french fries?" "Have you tried smoothies?"

No, I want to say. *No, but thank God you came along and suggested the one thing in the world I haven't tried to feed him, and the one thing he will miraculously eat.*

But I don't say this aloud, because they're just trying to help. They're not trying to make me feel worse than I already do. Meanwhile, Ezra must eat. This is not something I can just accept as part of who he is. He needs to eat to stay alive. So we receive a referral for another occupational therapist.

This time the therapist claims she knows what's keeping Ezra from eating. She explains that Ezra's sensory experience in his mouth is so convoluted that the best metaphor is a mouth shot full of Novocain. He has no idea where anything is in his mouth, so he relies on the same foods every time because they can't surprise him. He knows exactly what they will do. Imagine how terrifying it would be to put something in your mouth if you couldn't feel it in there, she says. I nod, excited to have finally found someone who seems to know what's going on.

For the rest of the session she pushes Ezra on the swing and makes him laugh. She's goofy with him the same way Patti is, in the way that he loves. She sings songs. She makes funny noises. All the while she gently encourages Ezra to accept a small rubber device into his mouth. He does accept it, even as I see his anxiousness, how defensive he is about anyone touching his mouth.

Before we leave, the therapist explains to me that eating is the most complicated human bodily process, matched only by sex. To eat we must use every aspect of our physiology, and this is why it can be so difficult for a kid like Ezra, whose sensory experience in his mouth is always misfiring. She hands me a printout that describes the forty-eight steps toward eating. I read each one: "Being in the room with aversive food." "Standing near aversive food." "Smelling aversive food." "Allowing aversive food on plate." I nod and nod, assuming she's right, assuming we've found the answer. This therapist is out of our insurance network. It costs $800 to have Ezra come here each month. We better have found the answer.

After just a month of weekly sessions, Ezra allows us to brush his teeth without crying or running away or even whining. But he still doesn't eat anything new.

EZRA COMES INTO the den carrying blue and yellow crayons and a pad of paper. This can mean only one thing. Michael and I exchange a look. Ezra pushes them toward me, and though I know what he wants, I say, "Ezra, use your words."

"Moose A. Moose and Zee?" he says.

"What about Moose A. Moose and Zee?" I ask. "What do you want me to do?"

"Use your words," Michael adds. We sound so dumb in these moments.

"Moose A. Moose and Zee?" Ezra says again.

I sigh and take the paper and crayons and draw the cartoon characters, which, if I don't say so myself, I've gotten pretty good at.

"Moose A. Moose, red shirt?" Ezra asks.

"Go find a red crayon," I tell him.

"Go find a red crayon," he repeats, and, hearing the words now that he's said them, he goes off to find one.

When he comes back with the red crayon, and I've drawn the red shirt, red pants, and red hat, he asks for a green shirt. I tell him to find a green crayon. And on and on we go, both of us learning to communicate with each other.

In September, he becomes ill once again. I call our old pediatrician, but she's not in today, so we make an appointment to meet with one of the other doctors there. She has long graying hair and a square body. She wears a denim jumper over tights. Griffin plays with toys on the floor, and Ezra lies in my arms. I explain to this doctor the strange pattern of Ezra's vomiting bouts that always come with low fevers. We discuss the various possibilities: the stress from all the moves, the constipation that's only now dissipating, the possibility that he has bacteria from the times he's touched his feces. At some point, I tell her

seven years old

that he's autistic, and her whole demeanor changes. She has an apologetic look on her face.

"Did you vaccinate him?" she asks, her head cocked in sympathy.

I don't want to answer her, because I know where this conversation goes. I did vaccinate him, partially and selectively. He never had the MMR. He never had a bad reaction. He never lost skills. He has always been who he is. How do I begin to explain to this person, someone I will likely not see again after today's visit, that I don't believe vaccines have anything to do with Ezra's autism? That instead I believe the thirteen epidemiological scientific studies that have shown that there isn't even a correlation between the two? I would never suggest that another mother might be wrong for believing vaccines harmed her child, because even as I believe the science, I also know that parenting is so individual, so completely none of someone else's beeswax. Why does this notion seem so hard for others to understand? Why the hell do other parents, doctors, strangers think it's acceptable to tell other parents what their kids need? I'm tired of the assumptions, of having to defend what I know to be true about my son, of having to tell a stranger, once again, that I know all about the alternative research and the anecdotes and the websites. I don't want to have to have this discussion just because I let slip that my son is autistic.

So I say, "I'd like to talk instead about how to help Ezra feel better."

She frowns. "Vaccinations might be directly related."

"I really don't think they are," I say as firmly as I can.

She stares me down. Finally, she takes a deep breath and presses the air through tight lips: judgment. I know it well. But at some point I have to stop worrying what others think about my choices with him, or that I'm a bad mother. At some point I have to stand on solid ground with Ezra, be willing to believe in what I see.

"Okay, then," I say after a moment. "If there's nothing else, I guess we'll just go home and wait for this to pass."

As we walk from the office the doctor says, "Only water, and no solids until he's held everything down for four hours. And then only crackers or dry toast."

I smile back at her. "I know," I say.

Some nights, I lie next to Ezra as he's falling asleep. I take in his profile, his lips, the soft fuzz above them, and the curve of his nose. He has a faint line on his nose like a lion or a cat, a linea nigra like the one I had on my belly when he was in my womb. Whenever I look at this line I'm reminded of what he is inside, the symmetry of his body, how he grew, a human animal, organs, bones, brain, blood, in two perfect halves inside me. I remember how we worked together behind the closed curtain of my skin, forming and form-ing, making him whole. How we did this fiercely intimate work together. Just he and I. How when my tiny animal baby came out, we stayed connected, skin to skin, mouth to nipple.

When I think of this I know why it feels so violating to have people tell me who my child is, or where his autism came from. It's private. It is no one else's business how he came to be.

Joint Attention

Michael and I have made no progress since leaving Massachusetts. We are comfortable living again in Portland. We know where we are and we can mingle once more with the friends we shied away from before we moved, when we were so terrified and lost concerning Ezra. But we are not magically happy now. We aren't suddenly romantic and affectionate. Michael is perhaps more depressed than he was in Massachusetts. He snaps at the kids. He ignores me. He walks heavily into the den to watch the game. We fight. He is always, always sick with headaches and colds and stomach ailments.

"I just want to be left alone," he tells me. "Is that too much to ask?"

It's just the move, I tell myself. *It will pass. It has to. The Michael I married will be back eventually.*

Meanwhile, I am still acting out familiar patterns. I distract myself with cute men on the streets, in stores, at the park. I make up elaborate fantasies where I do things I would never actually do, such as writing a note that I slip into the cute twentysomething guy's shirt pocket at the store: "I want sex, no strings. Meet me at six o'clock at Biddies Bar." It's ugly and desperate. It smacks of the old me, who elbowed past anyone to attract sexual attention from men. I still talk to Frank, but it's different now that we're not within driving distance of each other. Frank assumes he has to let go of the idea that we will wind up together, and I think I agree. I'm sharply aware that my wanting—for love, for connection—will always be mine. It likely wouldn't matter if Michael were more available right now. It wouldn't matter if Ezra weren't autistic or if I had no children. Sometimes I see clearly that I'm too in love with my longing to allow it to slip away, to truly release myself from its spiny grasp. Recognizing my promiscuous patterns changes them only so much. It means that I won't act out anymore, but it doesn't mean the longing goes away. And yet, sometimes just knowing that is enough. Sometimes accepting myself for who I am fills me. I wonder often if this alone is happiness—simply seeing myself clearly.

And then one morning, I call Michael at work.

"I want to talk about you moving out," I say.

"Kerry," he says, "no. I don't want that."

"I don't want to live with someone who doesn't love me," I say. I'm not being dramatic. I'm not projecting the ways I felt unloved as a child. This is what it feels like right now to live with Michael, and I've decided I don't want it. I can choose to be loved, and that's what I've decided to do.

"I do love you," he says. "It's me. I've been really down. I just haven't talked about it. But I don't want to lose you."

And so we begin, again, to talk about what's really going on. We're so bad at this, so slow. Our development as a married couple, as humans, is so erratic. Two steps back, and then one forward, and on and on.

seven years old

IN EARLY FALL, Ezra's speech therapist, Patti, calls me to tell me she thinks Ezra is hyperlexic. I know about hyperlexia, which is an exceptional ability to read words far above what would be expected at specific chronological ages, combined with a significant difficulty understanding spoken language. Hyperlexic children usually have a strong fascination with letters and numbers, as well as trouble with social skills. I already have considered whether Ezra is hyperlexic, but everything I have read made it sound as though a hyperlexic kid would be reading competently by two years old. I didn't realize it was a spectrum, like autism.

On a surface level, understanding that Ezra is hyperlexic is a breakthrough. It means we have this tangible way to support his learning and to help him in areas where he has challenges. It also helps him feel more in control in a world that surely must often feel unruly to him. Instead of saying, "It's time to shut off the computer and go to school," which he'll often ignore or cry about, his nanny or I can write the words and show them to him. He reads the words aloud, "Time to shut off the computer and go to school," and, like magic, he closes the computer and goes to the door.

We also use this tactic to encourage Ezra to speak more. If he says, "Outside," we can write, "I want to go outside," and he reads the words, we praise him, and then he is allowed to go outside. It also works when I want him to understand something: "You poured water on the computer, and the computer is broken now." The writing also benefits me. It calms me down and helps me to yell less when I'm angry.

I also use writing to persuade Ezra to answer yes. He uses the word "no" easily, but for some reason "yes" has come more slowly. He will say okay, but not yes. He can't yet say whether something happened, or if he likes something, but at the very least I'd like him to answer yes when I ask him if he wants something, like cookies, rather than simply repeating the word "cookies." So now when I ask him if he wants something, I hold up a sign with the words "yes" and "no." It works well. I tell the school about this tactic, and the two head teachers look at me oddly. One says, "We don't have a problem here with Ezra saying yes."

"Really?"

She laughs. "It took me so long to figure out what you were talking about, because it's not even remotely something he struggles with here." She describes how he yells out, "Yes!" when she asks if he wants to use the computer. I shake my head, laughing.

When I call Michael and tell him, I wait for the shock to pass before he speaks. "Sometimes I feel like I don't know my kid at all," he says. He doesn't say it unhappily, only with awe.

EVERY ONCE IN a while, Ezra poops in the bathtub and presses it between his fingers. Or he poops in the toilet and plays with it in the toilet water. Sometimes we find him in the back yard scooping up mud and putting it in his mouth. He shreds covers from his books and chews on the paper. He eats sand, dirt, muddy leaves. I say, "Ezra, stop. Take that out of your mouth," and he says, "Ah-choo!"

seven years old

Some things about Ezra remain so incomprehensible, so unfeasible, that the words used to describe them—pica, autism, sensory seeking—could not possibly describe what they really are, or what it really feels like for either him or us. When he acts out these behaviors, Michael and I yell at him. We put him in time-outs. We try to talk sense to him. We feel so unbearably upset. But we're less upset by the act than we are by how helpless we feel, how frightened we are, how much we can't know about what will come of these actions. We talk to each other often about being more patient. We want to do better. We want to be more accommodating of the fact that we won't always understand him or what he does.

Griffin, meanwhile, runs after Ezra. "Dezwa! What doing? Doing water, Dezwa? Doing mud?" I feel awful, hearing my words through Griffin's perspective.

ONE DAY I pick up Ezra at school and I find him giggling with another boy. They stand at the computer, where some golf game plays on the screen. They aren't playing the game, or rather they aren't playing the game in the way it was intended. The other boy hits the ball and words come up on the screen: "Out of bounds!" They yell out the words together, and then the boys explode into giggles. Two hyperlexic boys. Two boys with autism. Laughing and laughing about something only they would think is funny.

When I ask Ezra who his friends are, though, he names only girls. To be accurate, he doesn't answer the question "Who are your friends?" I talk and talk, trying to find the right combination of nouns and verbs that will lead him to give me an answer. Finally, I simply name the children in the school, and when I say the girls' names, he lights up and says them back. My feelings are bittersweet. He likes these girls, yes. Will they like him? I shouldn't let my mind wander here, I know, but my thoughts travel into the future when Ezra is a teenager, then an adult. Who will love my sweethearted boy?

In December, my mother and her husband, Charlie, visit. We go to the zoo, where the boys run and laugh. In the polar bear exhibit, water bubbles against the glass and Ezra presses his face close to watch their quick, lovely movement toward the water's surface. In the background, a polar bear takes three steps forward and then three steps backward, swinging his head as he does. It's a disturbing dance to watch. As we follow the kids, my mother tells me that Michael and I look so much better than we did in Massachusetts. She tells me Michael looked strange and puffy that week when we were in the hotel, waiting for the condo to be ready. She says his unhappiness was visible, like a costume.

I don't like to think back to that terrible month, how frightened we were, how lost. I don't like to be seen like this by my mother. I've always felt I had to protect my feelings from my mom, who feels the need to let me know she saw us a certain way, that she always sees me, she always knows. When I was a girl she would see me upset and say, "You're sad about the divorce" or, "You're afraid of what's coming

seven years old

next." It didn't matter if I told her she was wrong. She had decided what I was feeling, and in her mind, that was the only reality there was. So I learned to never let her see my feelings, to keep them safe from her ownership. I learned to not cry in front of anyone. I learned to keep my feelings close, inaccessible to most people.

I glance over at Michael now. He's imitating a monkey for Griffin, but also for Charlie and my mother. He needs them to think he's a good father, as if his continual concern for the kids and their happiness isn't obvious. He's always cared too much what other people think of him, even more so than I have.

Back at the house, Charlie watches Ezra's fast fingers on the notebook computer mouse, amazed. He is so good with Ezra, so kind and attentive. My mother points out this fact to me too often.

"Charlie is so good with the kids," she says. "He's such a good, caring man."

"I know," I tell her. "I can see that."

But she mentions it again, afraid maybe that if she doesn't, if she doesn't say the words aloud, my experience of him will be out of her control.

Charlie knows Ezra has an affinity for music and rhythm, so he suggests we buy Ezra an electronic keyboard. Not a child's keyboard, he says, an adult keyboard, on which Ezra can explore. So we buy one. Soon after, Ezra's school hires a music teacher. Ezra becomes his star student, one of the few who stays enthusiastic and engaged for the full hour. He quickly learns simple songs, which he plays for us and then beams with pride. Michael and I are so emotional seeing his pride, how good he feels about himself.

Over the next year, he will learn to read music. He follows his teacher's directions. He also learns to follow the rules of simple games, to catch a ball and throw it back. He joins me when I walk in a goofy way and stops when I stop. I can't help but note that these are all relationship development intervention skills, even though we never followed through with RDI therapy. I'm reminded of that notion out there that we must work fiercely with our autistic kids every day. That they need therapy to save them. Every therapy has testimonies on websites where parents say, "If it weren't for *xyz* therapy, I don't know where so-and-so would be." As always, we must do something do something or . . . or our kids will never be okay.

I'm not antitherapy. Not in the least. In truth, I think we all need therapy, and that includes our kids. I think children who have challenges need support around those challenges, and that certainly includes Ezra. But isn't it possible that if we love our kids, give them attention for what they do well, support them where they need help, and provide appropriate boundaries, they will progress on their own? Isn't it possible that it's not what we did or that they had such-and-such therapy, but that youngsters are astounding, resourceful creatures and they will find ways to be successful?

I'm also aware of how unfair it is how hard Ezra and kids like Ezra have to work to be acceptable and functional. Griffin doesn't

seven years old

have to do that. I want Ezra to just be a kid, to not have to constantly work on something that others need from him.

At some point I realize, but don't dare say out loud, so as not to jinx it, that Ezra is no longer having those vomiting episodes. All my guesses as to the reasons why are the same as before: Our household is no longer stressful; he's not playing with his feces anymore, and so there's less bacteria going into his mouth; he's not constipated anymore, and somehow this is related. I have no idea. Like so much else with Ezra, I don't have control.

Literal Thinking

Ezra still eats nothing, even with the optimism I've felt working with our most recent occupational therapist. I decide it's time to be more aggressive, and I speak to his therapist about the possibility of giving Ezra an SSRI medication for his anxiety around food. It's obvious to me at this point that Ezra knows how much everyone wants him to eat food. He's hypersensitive, actually, to those subtle emotions that come from another person. He also seems to really want to eat the food. He's fascinated by it. He loves books and TV shows about food. Often he asks for a certain food and I eagerly give it to him, only to have him set it down a moment later. Maybe, I think, if we can do something in his brain, mess around a bit with the electricity in there, it will be the final push into successful eating.

Some research indicates that children on the autistic spectrum have lower amounts of serotonin available in their brains. Of course, there's also research that they have too little vitamin D, too much vitamin D, glutathione, left brain–right brain connectivity, too many metals, not enough omega-3s, and on and on and on. But the anxiety-and-eating correlation makes sense to me, so I feel excited.

His therapist, however, is not onboard. She agrees that anxiety contributes to his eating issues, but she believes that the anxiety is a result of his sensory disturbances, and that if I let her continue working with him from that angle, eventually he'll eat.

I want her to understand. "He's my son. I need him to eat."

"I know," she says. "It must be so hard. But it takes a long time. I've had some clients for years."

I go home with the conversation in my head. I play a CD for Ezra and Griffin, hand them their milk and juice. Can I wait for years while Ezra keeps tolerating licks of artificially flavored lollipops, which is as much progress as he's made? It would be different, I suppose, if I knew for sure that Ezra's eating disorder was due to sensory disturbances, but I don't. I am doubtful, actually, that it is.

The following week, the therapist suggests that I withhold his milk until after he's eaten his meals. She uses this word "meal" with sincerity. She makes this suggestion as if Ezra's milk, with all its hidden supplements and vitamins, weren't the way I keep Ezra alive.

So, I speak with his doctor, have her do the research, and

LITERAL THINKING — 219
seven years old

we start a prescription of an antidepressant SSRI. Putting my son on medication isn't easy. I feel terrified and guilty. I'm conflicted about almost every decision I make for Ezra, and about this one, perhaps, I'm conflicted the most. It's different making decisions for Griffin, who, if I ask, will tell me how he's feeling and where. I can explain something to him, and he'll show me in a familiar manner that he understands. I'm so frightened of making Ezra suffer. I could not forgive myself if I ever made him suffer because I wanted him to do something to make me feel better. This eating issue is tricky. I need him to stay alive, so I need him to eat. That's my need. Is it also his? I don't know—can't know—what he needs.

After a few days on the medication, Ezra becomes ridiculously happy. He doesn't become hyper, as I feared he might, just happier, even, than he was before. At bedtime, his happiness notches up into mania. He runs through the house laughing. He rolls around on the bed, kicks the wall again and again. From our bedroom I hear Michael, who is usually the one putting Ezra to bed.

"Ezra! Enough! Go to sleep!"

Eventually, almost every night, Michael yelps in pain, having been clocked in the head by one of Ezra's manic errant movements, and stomps from the room. When I take over, I handle it even worse. I press his small body into the bed, yelling inane commands like, "Lie still! Close your eyes!"

After a couple weeks this side effect goes away and we are left with the positive results. He tolerates transitions so much better than before. He speaks more. He's less agitated in general.

But he still won't eat.

EVERY DAY AT three thirty in the afternoon, Griffin and I leave to pick up Ezra from school. We drive through the dark green Portland neighborhoods, past bike commuters, past cafés and lush native gardens, and onto the highway, where neon green ivy clings to the concrete walls that hold the cars in. Most of these days, Griffin complains about the drive. He wants to stay home, or he wants to go to the library, or he wants to go to the store. In the car, he finds things to complain about. He must use the phrase "I want" about a hundred times per day. I try to tell him in the car that I cannot pick up the toy he just purposely dropped on the floor, I can't read him the book he's holding, I can't take him out of his car seat or give him a hug, and I can't move him to sit in Ezra's seat, because I'm driving. I tell him that every day we do this same drive at the same time because we have to. Every day he complains. Why not sit back and enjoy the ride? Why not enjoy life a little more? But Griffin is who he is, and he will never be anyone else.

On the way home from Ezra's school, Griffin turns to Ezra.

"Dezwa, you have fun at school today?"

When Ezra doesn't answer, Griffin does what we do. He says, "Dezwa, yes or no?"

Griffin flips through a book, Ezra's favorite kind of book, an

seven years old

encyclopedia that has pictures and labels, such as flower and dog and fire truck. Earlier, Griffin cried and cried until finally Ezra handed over the book to his brother, accommodating him as usual. "Dezwa," Griffin says, "What's dat?"

When Ezra doesn't answer because he's busy listening to music, Griffin says, "Dat's right, Dezwa. It's a balloon. Good job. What's dat? Dat's right. It's a button."

Griffin sleeps with Ezra in his bed. This isn't negotiable if we want Griffin to go to sleep and then sleep through the night. Michael reads to them and they cuddle and hug. Once, I walked through the playroom and found Ezra kissing Griffin. He will not leave places without making sure Griffin also is leaving. Their relationship is private and warm. It is something that is all theirs, and I'm deeply grateful for it.

Most nights Michael falls asleep with the boys after reading them three books. Some nights, though, he makes it out of there. He climbs in beside me and seeks out my hand under the covers. We are still here. We are still doing this together. But we also still haven't had sex. It's been three years and counting.

One afternoon, Griffin comes to me crying because Ezra has pushed him away, rather than used his words. We have told Ezra repeatedly to use words. We have prompted him, role-played, given time-outs, and talked with him ad nauseam. But here he still is, pushing his brother. I sigh. What am I to do? It seems that it's time to explain to Griffin. So I empathize some, and then I just say it.

"Ezra's autistic, which means that he thinks differently than you do. And sometimes it means that he won't use his words, no matter how many times we encourage him to."

Griffin doesn't say anything. He's over it already, moving on. But I'm aware this is only the first of many conversations I might have with Griffin. Then again, maybe I won't. Maybe, like how he knew to say, "Dezwa, yes or no?" he'll just know who his brother is. He won't need someone to explain his brother to him.

THE SKY IS sharp blue with wispy clouds. A glinting plane moves slowly and surreally across it. Michael pulls the boys in their wagon as we head to the park. As usual, he walks fast, leaving me behind. It is one of his habits I despise, evidence of his insensitivity to me. In the past, I told him how it made me feel invisible, which is how I always felt as a child. I say nothing now. You can tell someone only so much. By now, he should think of it. I walk behind them, steaming, hurt, sick of the way some things never change. As we walk, I wonder how this happens in relationships, how sometimes you go places together and it is impossible to ever come back to a new place. There are some places you stay, walking the same walk, playing out the same patterns, and you are never able to swing back again. I fear this is what's happened with Michael and me. At some point, we crossed a threshold. We won't ever love in that way we did before. Our love has shifted permanently to something else, more like brother and sister than husband and wife.

seven years old

At the playground, I let it go, focusing instead on Ezra while Michael pushes Griffin on the swing. Ezra climbs the slide. When he comes down he still holds the sides, a flash of nervousness passing over his expression here and there. But the transformation between what he felt able to do last summer and what he's willing to do now is pretty extreme. He goes down again and again, and I clap for him. "You did it!" Anyone who doesn't know our story would think me one of those excessive parents who praise every banal thing their perfect son does.

When he's done with the slide, Ezra crawls into a tunnel in the play structure where a young girl, probably about two years old, and her father are playing.

"Hi there," the father says. "What's your name?"

Ezra, of course, doesn't answer. Instead, he leans in to smile at the girl, always too close, and then he hugs her.

I say to the man, "He's on the autistic spectrum, so he probably won't answer your questions. He hugs little girls a lot because he finds them cute, but he never hurts anyone. Let me know if you want me to intervene."

Even now, after all this time, I'm aware of how inaccurate words can be. I can't say, "He's on the autistic spectrum" without being afraid I need to explain that he's not violent, he's not scary, he's not contagious, he's not. In truth, I hate the expression "on the autistic spectrum." It's clunky, meaningless. But if I use the stripped-down alternative—autistic—without the qualifying idea of a spectrum, I fear people will envision the same images that came to me all those years ago when I first heard that word applied to Ezra. Maybe I shouldn't care. Maybe I should be less sensitive. But when it comes to my son, I can't seem to help it.

This time, luckily, the man needs no such qualifier. He tells me he teaches elementary school and he works with kids of all types. "No worries," he says. "Your son is fine in here with us." I let out my breath, thankful for these little mercies, for these people in the world.

I am sure that this is the night I have a dream about Ezra as a grown man. Or maybe it is after a similar day that summer when we went to the beach, when I again tagged behind Michael, who walked too fast, and Ezra went again and again to a pubescent girl and hugged her. She smiled and laughed at him and at her friend. I stood watching, my hand at my throat, and told him to stop, to come back here. I was too aware of his smallness, how he wouldn't always be small, and how someday other kids might not be so accepting of his odd behavior.

In my dream, Ezra is not small. He is in his early twenties, handsome and awkward, his dirty blond hair still too long. He tells me with detailed logic why he has the odd behaviors that he does. He searches for words some, like he does as a little boy, but his speech is more fluent. He's able to communicate. He talks on and on while I absorb what he says. When I wake up, I feel full, lit up, as though I've been gifted something enormous. I remember almost

LITERAL THINKING —225
seven years old

nothing the grown-up Ezra told me, only the fact that he could share himself verbally with me. It was just a dream, of course. It could mean nothing. But it could also be a visitation, a meeting on a different plane. I am convinced of so little in my life, but I want to believe Ezra knows himself like he did in the dream, and that now, somewhere inside, I know him like that, too.

THE AIR TURNS crisp, and the first rains arrive. September is still considered summer in Portland. It stays warm, no cooler than sixty-five degrees, and most days the sky is a blue sheet. I'm sharply aware of time passing. Ezra still doesn't eat. How many more years will we have this refrain? He doesn't eat, he doesn't eat. How long can a person stay healthy eating two foods and milk, as Ezra does? At his five-year well-child checkup, he weighed in at the seventy-fifth percentile for his age. His doctor and I laughed nervously, unsure how he defies all reason in this way.

One day, when I ask him if he wants milk, instead of saying okay, he says yes. Nothing preempting it. Nothing announcing his willingness to use a word he's refused his entire life. Just yes. Just like that. On another day, I leave my Facebook page up on my computer while I'm distracted doing something else. When I come back to it, I see that Ezra has opened a chat with a girl who is my Facebook friend because she likes my book. He wrote: "I will eat." The girl wrote back: "I'm sorry? You will what?" Oh my God. I write her quickly, telling her that my son wrote that and I apologize. I take a picture of the screen to show Michael later. We marvel over it, wondering what Ezra knows and doesn't know, wondering about our small son's mind.

I make a decision to pull Ezra out of his occupational therapy and try a new approach. There is research that suggests that autistic children limit eating because of neurological rigidity, not because of sensory confusion. This makes sense to me with Ezra. I was never convinced he wasn't eating solely because of sensory dysfunction. I make an appointment with a child behavioral psychologist at the university hospital, feeling not hopeful—an emotion I discarded long ago when it comes to Ezra's eating—but determined.

Our appointment with the psychologist is in the same location where we came years ago for that intern's botched attempt at speech therapy, and where the pregnant evaluator suggested I learn about pervasive developmental disorders (PDDs). I'm aware of how little the waiting area triggers me now, perhaps because Ezra's autism no longer feels like a shadowy monster. It is simply a part of who he is, and along with that, we need him to eat. He flaps his arms, laughs, and peers at the fish.

"Fish!" he says to me.

"Yes, I see the fish," I say. "Aren't they so pretty with their iridescent colors?"

I settle down with a magazine until we're called into the back. The psychologist says hello to Ezra and me. She tells me he's adorable, and then asks Ezra, "How about some toys?" She unlocks a cabinet and pulls out a tub of toys. There was a period of time when I would never have done this again. I would never have taken Ezra to meet another therapist, to sit on the floor of a sterile room with a small tub of toys, to expose him—and myself—once again to the evaluating eyes of another professional. Certainly, this therapist is lovely and clearly experiences Ezra as a little boy, not a case for her files. I am thankful for her, no question. But I've changed. I've moved into this life with my son. I'm not frightened anymore of what a therapist might say, what she might suggest about my child—that he is less than, that he is wrong, that he doesn't belong in our world. Finally, finally there is no longer a small part of me that is terrified these accusations might be true.

Here is Ezra: He communicates in ways I struggle to understand. He needs to learn to eat more foods. He finds rubber sea creatures in a plastic bag in a tub of toys and he lines them up in a row. He leans down so that he is eye level with them. He smiles and slides out the squid, which greets the other sea animals. "Hi, starfish," he says in a goofy voice. "Hi, octopus. Hi, bull shark. Hi, hammerhead shark."

The psychologist and I talk about Ezra's history with food and his behavior around food now. Ezra bounces a nubby sensory ball on the floors, the chair, the examination table, and then on the psychologist's and my heads.

She writes us up a basic plan for operant conditioning. I will offer Ezra a tiny piece of banana for five minutes. During the five minutes we can play with a toy, such as a puppet, that will eat the banana. When the puppet eats the banana, it receives the reward that we will also give to Ezra when he eats the banana. If he doesn't eat the banana after repeated sessions like this, I can offer that he lick the banana or hold it in his mouth. This will earn him the reward until he seems ready to move on to actually eating the banana.

I tell Michael about it later and we try to figure out a reward that will work. It should be his favorite thing, like his computer games. We can't imagine, however, taking away the one thing he adores, which he's had full access to for the past year, but it is what we would have to do to make the reward meaningful and effective. To take away his computer games would feel like punishment, and he hasn't done anything wrong. He doesn't intend to hurt himself or anyone else by not eating. So we feel a bit stuck.

I should note here that Michael and I don't limit Ezra's time on the computer. We let him do what he does on there—mostly play games—as much as he wants when he's home. A mother on that special-needs parenting board I used to frequent noted that she regretted letting her son spend all his time on the computer once he was older, but Michael and I decide to trust our instincts on this one. We believe Ezra receives more from the computer than he does from people.

An adult autistic I met online let me know that when parents take away that which makes an autistic person feel connected to something—which for Ezra is his computer—they devastate that person. Without his computer, Ezra feels disconnected. It's a world he understands, where he can feel successful. When he presses this button, that happens. Is that so terrible, that he feels more connected in some ways to what's on the screen than to people? Is it fair to presume that just because I want more human connection, he should too?

But we wind up not having to come up with a reward anyway, because by some stroke of luck, during this same week, Ezra's teacher at school makes progress with him. She has figured out that if she tucks him under her arm and allows him to lie back—as though he were a baby again—and sings a song about bananas that they make up together, he will allow the banana into his mouth. She feeds him small mashed-up pieces with her fingers. They sit in the kitchen by themselves, away from the other kids and hubbub, in front of a window where Ezra can witness the back yard. I arrive early one day and the other teacher, Kelly, brings me back to the kitchen to see, and it makes me uncomfortable: the way he lies back against his teacher, the way he looks out the window as though in a dream, her fingers going into his mouth. Something about it reminds me of those ancient therapies alternative practitioners did, still do, such as "holding therapy," which led to a girl's being suffocated. But by the end of two weeks, he will sit up and eat a whole banana, as long as the teacher holds it, so I push those discomforts aside.

When I take him back to the psychologist, though, he squirms and complains and will only touch the very tip of his tongue to a tiny piece of banana. At home, he is the same way. This is typical of him. He is environment-specific with his behaviors. His teacher assures me he eventually will generalize to other environments. She reminds me that he eventually answered yes at home, long after he was doing it in school. Meanwhile, she has moved on to encouraging him to take small bites of macaroni and cheese, and she told me she also plans on persuading him to accept one green vegetable. For the most part, I'm not worried. It is enough to know that my son is eating some fruit and a little protein.

But then things about Ezra's school begin to concern us. One thing is that the teachers have no qualifications to work with special-needs children. A mother-daughter team, they have a son and grandson of their own who is autistic, but they haven't received any formal training. When the parents start asking about the staff's educational credentials, we hurt their feelings. Hurt? Why is it our problem that they feel hurt? A few of the parents and I exchange some emails to discuss this response. These are our children. This is the school we pay. We want trained teachers. One day, a teacher tells us excitedly that they will have a speech therapist coming in to help out on Thursdays. This makes the parents happy, but in two weeks, she is gone again. No one tells us anything. At some point, one of the parents asks what happened to her, and the teacher says, "Oh, Kelly didn't like her trying to tell her what to do."

"But she's a speech therapist," the parent said. "She knows what she's doing, right?"

"It didn't work for us to have anyone else here, stepping on our toes."

We begin to notice that only immediate family works at the school: the mother and grandmother teachers, and now a hired-on sister for afternoons. They have a music teacher we love, but soon enough, he disappears. And, again, we are told nothing. This time, I ask about it. Kelly's face scrunches with anger. "Let's just say he was no longer doing his job." I don't dare ask more.

The idea that perhaps we haven't found a place for Ezra to land, that we might have to search again for a school where he can thrive, makes Michael and me feel like dying. We can't go there yet. No way. Not after everything we went through to wind up here. No, no, no. The other parents have stories, too—public schools that offered almost nothing to their children, special education classrooms that had no resources, schools that treated their children like burdens to the system. They feel like Michael and I do. The teachers at Ezra's school know this. Every child that starts there comes with a parent who says, "Thank God for you. I don't know what else we would have done." Over time, the teachers need to hear more of this. They rely on it. If we give any feedback that suggests they might not be perfect, they remind us that we need them. There is nothing else for us. The implication is that we have no choice but to send our children to their school.

Every day when I pick up Ezra, he is on the computer, playing games that are beneath his ability. I don't mind this so much.

I figure he's been doing other things there as well, and hopefully more than just the worksheets for recognizing letters and numbers that someone has photocopied from a preschool book. I sit down next to him, Griffin clinging to my leg. Griffin has hit a phase in his life where he's nervous about other children. Where most kids have a normal period of separation anxiety that corresponds with their ability to move around on their own, and that resolves somewhere around eighteen months, Griffin has continued to feel anxious into his second year. He wants to be around other children. He watches everything they do, but he is afraid to join in. I'm not particularly worried about it. Ezra has taught me many things, the least being that kids are unique. All I can do as Griffin's mother is help and support him as he moves through the world with his fear. So, he holds tight to me while we wait for Ezra to finish up this particular game so we can leave.

One day, while doing exactly this, a bunch of other children are in the room. Two are brothers, one of whom was the one that fell on the floor, laughing and playing with Ezra, many months ago. The brothers are roughhousing on the floor, kicking each other. The teachers sit on chairs. Kelly says, "Cut it out, you two."

They don't.

She says, more loudly, "Hey! Cut it out!"

They don't.

She grabs a thin children's paperback book that sits on the

table next to her, folds it over, stands up, and swats both their legs. "Stop it, now!" she says.

I don't say anything. I don't do anything. I'm not sure what I've seen, in that same way that someone might not know what she saw while watching magic performed. What just happened? Is it what I thought? Is there some trick I missed?

I gather up my children. I drive home. I call Michael and tell him. Then I call those boys' mother. I do not know her well, but I know her somewhat. We've had a few pleasant chats while waiting for our kids to finish something up before leaving school. I tell her what I saw because I would want to know if someone saw that happening to my children. At first, she goes silent. Then she says. "I'm sure Kelly meant no harm."

"What are you going to do?"

"I'll ask her about it. But I'm sure it wasn't anything."

"She smacked your kids' legs," I say. "It's a school. And kids like ours are more likely to be physically abused than other kids."

"Oh, yeah," she says. "But I'm sure she didn't mean any harm."

The following day, Ezra has a cold and doesn't make it in to school. But the day after that, I bring him. I leave Griffin with his nanny. Kelly sees me coming and turns around. She makes a noise and stomps out of the room. Her mother says, "I don't think she's ready to talk to you yet."

"Not ready to talk to me yet?" I ask, incredulous.

The mother has long, graying hair. She wears tie-dyed shirts and is often barefoot, which a few parents have wondered about regarding the health code. Michael refers to her as Soaring Spirit, which is the name she uses for her professional email address.

"The other mother spoke with her and told her she knows it's fine and that she didn't mean anything by it. She's hurt," Soaring Spirit says.

I almost laugh. I help Ezra take off his jacket and let him settle in, and then I go to find Kelly.

When I do, she's in the kitchen by herself. She says, her mouth tight, "If you don't trust me, then don't bring your son here."

"Are you kidding me?"

"I don't want to talk to you right now," she says. "I'm too upset."

"Well, I need to talk to you," I say. "I'm upset, too. I saw something and I need to know it won't happen to my son."

She glares, wide-eyed, as though I've said something outrageous. "It won't!" she says. "Ezra's a different kind of kid."

I can't even respond. My child is not the kind of kid you hit? What does that even mean?

"Besides," she says, "I only did it because Griffin is so nervous all the time. I feel like I have to keep the others kids calm around him."

"You're saying you hit those boys because of my two-year-old? You're blaming Griffin for your behavior?" I can't modulate my voice. My anger is big. But I'm also aware of what Michael said: Don't do anything you can't take back. As long as Ezra is there, we don't want them taking out their feelings about you on our son.

seven years old

By now, Kelly's mother, Soaring Spirit, has joined us.

"Honey," she says. She puts a hand on my shoulder. "She's hurt. Give her some time."

I don't say what I want badly to say, that I'm quite sure she's not the one who's hurt here. It's those kids she should be worried about. But I do say, "Isn't this a school? Is it really professional to feel hurt by a parent's feedback?"

"Sweetie," Soaring Spirit says, "we can't help it when we feel hurt. This is a family more than a school. A family of families who are in this battle together. We have to take care of one another, not treat each other like corporate suits."

I am so completely at a loss, so shocked and in disbelief, I just leave. And Michael and I immediately start fretting about finding Ezra another school.

I begin an email exchange with some other mothers at the school who feel like I do. We want out. We don't like this feeling of being held captive by a school simply because our children are on the autistic spectrum. There are hundreds of schools in the metro area. Why would we think there is only one school that works with children like ours? And now it turns out that crazy, controlling women who feel hurt all the time run that one school. The parents meet for coffee. We bitch and laugh. We declare we're on a mission together to find another school.

Two of the mothers have sons who are higher in their functioning. They are more verbal, more conversational. They will both be rediagnosed as having Asperger's syndrome later that year. They find typical schools that welcome quirky kids into classrooms. Three of us have sons who are not quite so functional. This issue of functionality is difficult to pin down. Most people assume high-functioning means verbal, more connected, and able to do self-care. They assume low-functioning people are nonverbal, struggle with self-care, and are unable to connect with others. The problem with these understandings is that they are often completely inaccurate. A very verbal person with Asperger's may never have a job or live independently because he can't learn social behavior, or because some sensory issue is too much in the way for him. But a person who may appear more autistic—rocking, flapping, not making eye contact—may write eloquently and articulately, and may lead an organization that works for the rights of autistic people.

My son could be classified as high-functioning in some areas. The behavioral psychologist we saw noted that once Ezra resolves his speech difficulties, he'll be on par with people with Asperger's syndrome. Indeed, researchers have noted that the differences between high-functioning autistic people and people with Asperger's become negligible after a certain point in development. But it's hard to tell if Ezra will ever catch up in his language. And what does that even mean, to catch up? Do people with autism "catch up," or do they learn to modify their behaviors enough to fit in better with a society that won't accommodate them?

Also, I worry about such classifications and how they draw lines between people. I see it among some mothers, how they need their child to be diagnosed with Asperger's, rather than autism. Some adults with Asperger's syndrome want Asperger's to be its own issue, separated from autism. They feel they are perhaps better than those who can't attain such a diagnosis. Parents whose children are more severely affected claim that it's easy for those with Asperger's to say they don't want to be recovered or cured, because they aren't so dysfunctional. The levels of functioning, however, are so much more complex than that.

The other parents and I discuss these issues. Where is that line between being functional and being oneself? How do we help our children navigate such a line? It is such a relief to have other mothers to talk with, mothers who understand. After all this time, I feel seen by other people again. I feel like at least some of these parents are friends. I confide in a couple of them about what is happening to my marriage: how I am beginning to see that Michael and I may have destroyed our relationship to the point where we are just friends. I'm giving it this year to see what happens, to see if anything changes. Or, like everything else in my world, if it stays the same shape and it's my job to simply acknowledge it for what it is.

* * *

Central Coherence

On a Saturday while the weather is still nice, I leave Michael with a napping Griffin and take Ezra in his red wagon to the park. Ezra sits patiently as he always does, his floppy blond hair lifting slightly with every bump we ride over. If Griffin were here he'd be chattering away about the park, the flowers, the doggies, the houses. Griffin talks and talks. It's who he is. Ezra is a different kind of guy. This is something my boys help me grasp: I am me. Michael is Michael. Griffin is Griffin. And Ezra is Ezra. There's nothing we can do about it. Nor, really, should there be.

I try to steer us past the baseball diamond, but to no avail. Ezra sees it immediately. He loves the powdery dirt that explodes into clouds when he throws it in the air. He loves the slippery white chalk that, no matter how many times he kicks it or runs his fingers through it, is there in thick new lines next time we come. I used to try to redirect him, to force him to leave the field of dirt and go to the playground, where there are swings and a slide and a sandbox. He had an emotional fit almost every time. At some point, I stopped this nonsense of trying to force him to play in a way that felt more comfortable for me. Besides, if I just allow him a few minutes to play with the dirt, he eventually makes his way over to the playground equipment. I'm learning, I'm learning. I'm slow, but Ezra teaches me, bit by bit, to be better at this.

Today, there is a father and son practicing hitting baseballs.

seven years old

The son, maybe a year or two older than Ezra, is suited up in full Little League attire, and the father wears a catcher's mitt. I hear him say comments to his son such as, "Hold your arms up a little higher. There you go. That's good." He pitches to the boy, and the boy hits a ground ball that the father chases, yelling praises. My heart quickens.

"Ezra!" I call, but he is already ahead of me. He finds himself a spot near where the boy and his father play and drops to his knees. He digs his hands inside the dirt. I can see the father glancing at Ezra. They keep playing, but I know that Ezra is in the way, and they were there first. I move closer and crouch down next to Ezra. "You can't play in the dirt today, buddy. They're playing baseball here."

Ezra whines and turns around, hoping I'll leave him alone. I meet the father's eyes. He wears an expression I recognize well. It's the what's-wrong-with-that-kid expression. Or, more accurately, it's the I'm-glad-my-kid-isn't-like-that face. Or even my-kid's-better-than-yours. I try to be patient with this. If Ezra weren't who he is, if I didn't love him with that fierce animal love we all feel for our children, I might have feelings like that, too. Maybe I'd see disabled children and think, *How sad. I'm so blessed my child isn't like that.* But that's not what my life became. My life is one where I had Ezra, where I sat beside my strange beautiful boy who grew up and showed me that there is nothing sad about my life. That I'm just as blessed as any other parent. That Ezra's social oddities and funny mannerisms are part of a whole constellation of behaviors and thoughts and approaches that fill my life, that make me see differently than I might have otherwise. I'm happy with that. I'm lucky, even.

Eventually, I have to pick up a dirt-covered Ezra, who is now crying in frustration, and carry him off the baseball field. I don't waste time looking at that father again.

This same afternoon, Ezra figures out how to open the child-proof lock I put on the front door and walks outside. He wanders into the garage across the street, where our neighbor is working on a project, and the neighbor walks him back to us. I apologize and thank him When Ezra and I are inside, I crouch down to his eye level.

"You don't ever walk out of this house on your own. Do you hear me? Not ever."

He tries to look away. He is almost smiling, which angers me more.

"This isn't funny, Ezra! You can get hurt out there. You can get lost. You can't do that again!"

He looks right at me and says, "Ah-choo!"

Tears sting my eyes. Sometimes the helplessness is over-whelming.

I take him to his room and make him sit on his bed. "Sit there!" I yell. "Just sit there!"

Finally, he cries. I wanted a reaction, and I got one. I go into the bathroom and splash water on my face. I lean into the mirror and tell myself to calm down, that yelling doesn't help anything. I go back to Ezra's room, where I find him crying.

seven years old

"Do you want a hug?" I ask.

He comes to me and wraps his small arms around my neck. I hold him until he lets go.

"I'm sorry," I whisper.

I wake one morning, a few weeks later, to Ezra climbing into my bed.

"I love you," he says in his halting robot speech. It is the first time he's used those words with me.

"Get over here and give Mommy a kiss," I say.

He laughs and kisses the wall. It's a game we made up.

"Don't kiss the wall. Kiss Mommy!" I say.

He laughs and kisses the lamp. Then the TV. Then the dresser. And on until, finally, he comes and gives me my kiss.

ONE WEEKEND MORNING after Michael has slept through the night with the boys or in the guest room, as he tends to do most evenings, he comes into the bedroom where I sleep. "I'm guessing Ezra is in here with you."

I sit up. He's not. He's not here.

I jump up, throw on a robe, and follow Michael upstairs. He checks the guest room, opens closets. Last night Ezra got up in the middle of the night. He does that sometimes, is woken by Griffin or wets his bed, and then he can't fall back to sleep. He came to my bed completely naked, having taken off his wet pajamas. I got up to re-dress him in a new nighttime diaper and pajamas. Then he started giggling and tossing around, thinking about one of his video games. I kicked him out of my bedroom, wanting to sleep, assuming he would go play and then eventually make his way back to bed, like he does on most nights he wakes up. But now I see I should never have done that. I never should have sent my small five-year-old boy out on his own in the middle of the night. What was I thinking? What kind of mother am I?

He isn't in any closets or the bathroom or in a cabinet or under blankets. I open the door that leads to the garage, and there is the diaper I put on him and the pajama bottoms. He took them off here, inside the garage, closing the self-locking door behind him. In the garage, everything that was there before is the same: the stroller, the stack of old paint pails, the boxes, the bunched-up area rug. My heart is pounding. It is hard to imagine that I was sleeping a moment ago, and now I feel like I will never sleep again. This is how things happen, of course. One moment life is one way, and then the next it is another way entirely. Like Ezra's conception, like autism in our lives. It just *is*, and everything that came before is a whole other existence. I look at photographs now of the me who was there before Ezra, before motherhood, and I can't imagine who she is. This is what life would be like if Ezra were gone. It would be incomprehensible. I can barely say that word: gone. It cannot be. We must find him. We must.

Michael opens the garage door, raising the curtain on pouring rain. It isn't possible that Ezra could have opened the garage door, pressing the button to do so, and then closed it again from outside. The car, which has a remote for the door, is locked. It isn't possible, and yet Michael and I have lost all sense of logic. Anything is possible. We must find our son.

"He's not out here," Michael says, the desperation thick in his voice. "I don't see him."

And in that moment, the area rug moves. I breathe out. Ezra pushes the heavy rug off of him. He has curled up inside it and fallen asleep, like a wild animal looking for warmth. It is almost an optical illusion. In one moment it is one way, and in the next moment it is another. Had I looked more closely, had I looked the right way, I would have seen him more accurately.

"Bath," he says.

Michael picks him up. I press my face against Ezra's. He smells like old, musty rug.

"Ezra," I say. "Ezra," bringing him back here with his name.

Emotion Recognition

On a daily basis, here are some details about Ezra that nag at my brain:

When he poops, he wipes himself with toilet paper, like he should, but then he leaves the toilet paper hanging on the roll. Sometimes, instead of toilet paper, he uses whatever towel is hanging on the rack, only to be discovered later when one of us goes to dry our hands.

He doesn't eat.

He can't have a conversation.

He's never been to the dentist.

I cannot begin to imagine how a dentist visit would go. Ezra barely lets us into his mouth to brush his teeth. When he was two years old, we just didn't brush them. When he was three, about once per week, Michael—always the braver of the two of us—would wrestle a screaming Ezra to the floor and force him to accept the brush into his mouth. When he is four and five years old, we warn him the brushing is coming, and then we count to five on each side while he doesn't cry, but wears a look of being tortured. Sometimes it works to make him laugh. I tell him to shake his body around until all those wiggles are out and he can stay still while I brush. So he does it, laughing—shake, shake, shake—and while his mouth is open from giggling, I reach in there. We use a pinprick's amount of toothpaste, or he'll gag and scream and won't let us in at all. Our only salvation is that he's inherited my teeth, the teeth of Eastern European Jews, who have survived all sorts of devastation and deprivation. He has hearty genes. Thank God for that.

Having my new friends helps. I share our story about teeth brushing, and they each have one of their own. One wrangles her child to the floor. Another waits until her child is dead asleep (which is brilliant—I file it away for future use). Another admits that she brushes her kid's teeth about once a week, if that. One tells us about her dentist, whom she calls the "tooth whisperer." We all reach into our purses for pens so we can write down the name.

When we go to the dentist, I bring Griffin, hoping they can take a peek in his mouth, too. I tried role-playing with Ezra, even bought him a book about going to the dentist, but, as with so many other concepts with him, I had no idea whether he understood. I told him this morning that we were going to the dentist, and he happily left. In the parking lot, I turned around and said, "Ready to see the dentist, Ezra?"

He said, "Yes."

And Griffin said, "I want to see the dentist!"

"Great," I told him. "You can see the dentist."

Inside we walk by the elevator, even though we are heading to the third floor. Ezra will not ride on elevators. He finds them freaky. In a year or so he'll be over this phobia, but for now, we climb the stairs. I am winded by the time we reach the third floor. The waiting room has neon lights overhead in the shape and hues of a rainbow, and primary-colored bleachers along the side of the room meant for children's play. Ezra points up at the light, and he and Griffin climb up and down the structure.

When the doctor comes out, he sits with me first to chat. I tell him Ezra is autistic. I tell him about our tooth-brushing battle. And I tell him my fears about being here. He smiles and nods, and at one point pats my knee like a grandpa. He is like Mr. Rogers in a white coat. I love him instantly.

We go into the back, where there are rows of dentist chairs that look more like massage chairs, all flat with lights overhead. The doctor shows me the room where they let kids who have become upset cool off. It has a TV and some books. While we're in there, Ezra prances off into the main room, where the other dentists work on children in the chairs.

"Ezra!" I call, but Dr. Rogers—not his real name, but a perfect alias—shakes his head.

"It's fine," he says. "Let him go. We want our kids to feel comfortable here."

They have a Wii console and a tiny TV in the main area, which we also have at home and is one of Ezra's favorite pastimes. Ezra starts playing, jumping around and spinning, and just generally getting in people's way. I try to make him stop, but again Dr. Rogers touches my arm as if to say, *Relax, Mama*.

When we do settle in for a checkup, Ezra is willing to lie back. He's willing to play with the water thingy and the suck-up-the-water thingy, but he won't let Dr. Rogers look in his mouth for more than a few moments. Dr. Rogers tells me it's more important that Ezra have a good association with the dentist than it is that he sees into his mouth, so we decide to reschedule. Griffin, who has clung to my leg this whole time, is too scared as well. The nurse shows me a four-ounce tube of some special-order, mild-tasting toothpaste for Ezra, which I buy for twenty bucks.

"Thank you so much," I tell Dr. Rogers on our way out.

"Nothing to thank me for, unfortunately," he says, referring to the fact that Ezra's checkup was incomplete.

But he has no idea how truly thankful I am.

We go back every three months, and on the third visit, Dr. Rogers' son, an equally kind man, examines Ezra's mouth long enough to see that he has two pretty bad cavities. We set up two more appointments. One is called an anxiety-reduction session, where they will go through the motions of the procedure, and the next is the real deal.

It is in these mundane moments—taking my child to the dentist, and then to have a cavity filled—that I'm most aware of how different parenting Ezra can be. I know that even as Griffin is too nervous just yet to let the dentist see inside his mouth, eventually he will. And he does. In the future, Griffin will enjoy the whole process. He'll like when the assistant calls the tools funny names and he does what she says and then leaves with a little toy. He will also need a crown when he's newly four. He'll ask me whether it will have jewels. And he'll derive great pleasure from wearing the "You're the Boss at Dr. Rogers'" bracelet and accepting the nitrous and opening his mouth wide to have the crown fitted on his tooth. But for Ezra, I never know what he understands.

At the anxiety-reduction appointment, Ezra seems to like the

nitrous. He reaches for it when they take it away and says, "More."
On the day of the actual procedure, I'm nervous about how this will
go; but I also know that so many times I've felt worried and he's had
a great time. It's such a crapshoot with him. Because I know Ezra
will require more attention, I leave Griffin at home with the nanny.
We check in and are taken to one of the chairs in the big room. They
roll over the nitrous station, and I tell them the story of what happened when we came for the preparation session, how Ezra's surely
a future drug user, and we laugh. Then the dentist—Dr. Rogers'
son—comes over to do the work. He completes one tooth, and all
seems to be going well enough, until Ezra pushes the gas off his
face, sits up, and pukes on my jeans.

The doctor and assistants move quickly to clean it up. They use
that odor-killer all pediatric offices have to treat carpets that are
barfed on. I try to help, embarrassed, but they say no, no, it happens
sometimes with nitrous. Some kids are sensitive to it. While this
happens, Ezra gets the hell out of there. We are so caught up with
cleaning the carpet and my pants that we don't notice, until one of
the assistants asks, "Where did he go?" We all walk a couple steps
to see him on the Wii, laughing and jumping around.

The doctor looks at me. "Do you think we should try again, or
is that enough for now?"

I shake my head. "Let's let him be."

He moves on to another patient, but before we leave he checks
in with me about a plan. I don't want Ezra on the nitrous again if

it makes him sick, and he agrees. He suggests the possibility of general anesthesia instead, which he tells me they've done with a number of kids who don't do well with the local, and who also have special needs that make such procedures difficult.

Later, Michael and I decide the general anesthesia would be best. They could fill the cavity and also clean his teeth, give him a fluoride treatment, and put sealants on his teeth. The downside, as usual, is the cost. We will have to pay close to $3,000, and because the procedure doesn't require anesthesia—that is, it wouldn't if Ezra didn't have the issues he does—insurance won't cover it. So we set the appointment and liquidate the small amount of stock we have.

The day of the procedure, Michael takes him. I'm so anxious I have to take a Xanax. Michael calls me to keep me apprised of what's happening. He tells me that Ezra didn't even feel the anesthetic shot, and then he fell asleep on Michael's lap. Later we learn that the tooth wound up being in bad enough shape that they pulled it, so he would have needed the heavy anesthesia anyway. They did the rest of the procedure we wanted done as well. By the time they arrive home, Ezra is still sleeping heavily, so we lay him in our bed. I lie next to him to watch him a bit. A few times he moves his tongue around, feeling the spot in his mouth where there's no tooth anymore. I ask him how he's feeling, but he falls back asleep. An hour or so later he stands up and starts weaving around the house.

"Whoa, whoa," he says.

"Are you dizzy?" I ask him.

"Yes."

I help guide his body so he doesn't walk into walls.

Michael has to force him to take a little Tylenol with codeine so he won't be in pain, but the process of forcing him to take the medicine is painful in its own right. He is so upset he invariably gags. But at least it is in him—until six hours from now, when we'll have to do it again.

WE GO TO the science museum often, where the kids can press levers and play with water and sand and a homemade slime substance called flubber. Michael and I have to go together because the museum is huge and often crowded, and rarely can we convince the kids to stay in the same area. We park and go in with our membership card, and then we basically have to say goodbye to each other. Today, I'm the one with Ezra. Michael and I agree about how different it is to be with Griffin. There is a sense of ease that comes with having Griffin in public that we can't have with Ezra. At Ezra's age, there are behaviors people expect that Ezra can't always come through on. For instance, he might pour sand on your toddler's head to see what will happen. Don't take it personally. He will also pour it on his own. He might say something meaningless to you or your child. He might take your child's flubber off her tray because he wants it. He might step over your child's tower without thinking, knocking down your kid's hard work. He might reach into one of the fish tanks and try to grab one of the fish. We have to stay constantly on top of him so as to ward off such events, hopefully before they happen. But they do happen, they do.

On this day, I have to head into the sandpit without taking my shoes off—aware of the tsk-tsks from other mothers—so that I can stop Ezra, who is raising a colander up to see what happens when the little streams of sand angle down onto the small blond child near him.

When I step out of the sandpit, trauma successfully averted, a slim mother who's seen the whole thing laughs.

"Good job," she says.

I shake my head and laugh with her. "I hate this place," I say, and she smiles. We chat a bit. She points out her kid, a cute boy with shaggy brown hair who runs a dump truck along the edge of the enclosed sandbox. I mention how all the fathers who come here look downtrodden and defeated. She agrees, musing that the new world order, where dads actually help moms take care of the children, hasn't done a ton for the men. We laugh again. A little more chatting, and I tell her my son is autistic. When he was a toddler I rarely felt the need to tell strangers. Now, however, his differences are so obvious, I know they'll wonder, and I don't like the idea of their wondering. Telling them first is a sort of defense mechanism.

"Oh," she says, "have you tried the dolphin thing?"

Oh boy. "The dolphin thing?" I ask.

"I have a friend who has a friend who has a child with autism, and she took her to a place in California where dolphins work with children with autism. Apparently, dolphins are the only other creatures that speak the same language."

"I really don't believe in that sort of stuff," I say.

"But it's true! My friend said her friend's daughter is recovered now. You should look into it."

"Okay," I say. "Thanks." Luckily, this is when Ezra decides to come out of the sandpit. I lean down to help him put his shoes on, which breaks my eye contact with her and, therefore, also her need to keep talking to me about it.

"Good luck," she says as we walk away.

In the arts and crafts room, children write wishes on construction paper leaves and hang them on the wishing tree. While Ezra plays with the flubber, I grab one of these leaves and write: *I wish for a world that will welcome my autistic son.* I fasten the ribbon and tie it to the tree.

MICHAEL AND I stand in the kitchen one evening, discussing the situation with Ezra's school, how we need a new one, and he sighs, overwhelmed, and says, "I'd do anything to have Ezra not be autistic."

My heart stops. *Don't say that,* I want to tell him. *It's not fair to Ezra. He can't help who he is.* But that instinct is more like habit. Our lives are different now. The panic about whether Ezra will be okay is gone. Ezra is who he is, and this level of honesty between

Michael and me is hard won. And also, I understand. Sometimes I feel that way too.

Other parents don't have to do what we do, searching their cities for a place where their unique child can learn in the way he learns, a place that is supportive but challenging, a place where we can trust he will be safe. What I want for Ezra more than anything else in the world is for him to be happy, to feel good about who he is. I want so much for him not to judge himself the way his father and I constantly judge ourselves, the way the world seems to judge autistic people. Everything I do, I know, has to be about that goal. Yet it's so hard to know where the balance is between helping him do what he needs to express himself in the world, to not be taken advantage of, hurt, squashed, silenced—and also helping him know he is perfect to me as he is. Don't all children need to know they are perfect in their parents' eyes? That their parents wouldn't trade them for anything?

Every few months, I still talk to Frank. I admit that I miss him. Or maybe I just miss feeling like someone wants me that badly. I'm pretty sure Michael's and my marriage is over. Whatever intimacy we've regained, I'm pretty sure it's too late. Something has passed. I won't dare say that at this point. I won't dare admit it to myself. But somewhere inside I know the end of us is coming, and so talking to Frank is how I know to feel better.

"Do you believe that people can change?" he asks me.

I know he asks this because he's not in love with his wife, and he wants to be. It would be so much better for him. He comes from a family that would never understand if he chose to leave her, this lovely, giving person who has sacrificed so much for him. But I can't help thinking of my own situation. I would like to figure out how to be the sort of person I'm not, someone more, perhaps, like Frank's wife, someone who wouldn't be on the phone right now with a man who isn't her husband. Also, I think of Ezra. How can I not think of Ezra? Of whether all the therapies we force him into will really make a difference. Of whether the therapies have to make a difference for Ezra to be worthwhile in the world.

"I don't think so," I tell Frank now, my most honest answer.

"But you're a therapist," he says. "How can you not believe in people's ability to change?"

"Therapy isn't surgery. You can't remove parts of who you are."

"Then what? Why go?" He's in therapy, I know, so I can hear his frustration.

"I think the best we can do is know who we are. Really know who we are and do our best to not judge that. I think that's the closest we can come to contentment."

"What does this mean for me, then?" he asks. "Do you think I'll ever be able to be happy with my wife?"

"You know I can't answer that for you."

He's silent a moment. I can hear him breathing. "Often I fear I chose her because she's the kind of woman my family approves of and I want them to approve of me, too."

"It's so hard, isn't it?" I say. "How are we supposed to find who we really are and what we really need when there are so many pre-scripted ideas already clogging our psyches?"

I think again of Ezra, about my fear that the world will never accommodate his strangeness. My fear that he will always be pushed to the outskirts, a freak, or swallowed whole, expected to be like all autistic children, whatever that is. He will always be labeled, compartmentalized, judged, never able to be just himself.

One afternoon, a friend I've made through Ezra's school, Julie, calls with some news. One of the parents who left Ezra's school because it couldn't accommodate her son's needs is starting a school of her own. It sounds like the real deal. I contact the parent and schedule a lunch meeting for Julie and me. The school directors tell us about their plans: qualified teachers, training, a structured curriculum, involved therapists. Julie and I look at each other, thrilled. No wacky approaches, such as the one Soaring Spirit used to help Ezra feel like he was a baby again. No barefooted teachers without qualifications. No swatting children with books. Just empirically supported approaches to working with children on the autistic spectrum.

As summer approaches, we figure it is time to take Ezra out of the other school. The new school is under way. We have received material and an application. They have hired real, credentialed, experienced instructors and therapists. They have a classroom inside another school and so have access to all the resources—the art room, the occupational therapy room, the kitchen, and the gym. The only problem is that it is going to cost us the equivalent of college tuition. But we have to find a way. We have to.

We talk to friends and family. Someone says to us, "Lots of people send their children to expensive private schools."

Michael shakes his head. "This is different," he says. "Those people are choosing to send their children to a school because they want a certain kind of education for them. Either we do this or our kid gets fucked by the public school system."

That person laughs. "Come on, there are other places to send him."

We just stare at this person. "Show us where," one of us says. "Please. We'd love more options."

That person says nothing.

Ezra turns six. We throw him a small party, but he mostly stays in his room with the door closed and plays on his computer. An autistic friend on Facebook tells me she wishes when she was a child that her parents had allowed her to stay in her room during the parties they threw her.

I write an email to my parents, begging them for help with the new school's tuition, and they both throw in some cash. When I thank them, wishing words weren't so paltry, my father says, "It's Ezra."

It's Ezra.

So we arrange for him to start at the new school. We also arrange for Griffin to start preschool at the school in which Ezra's school is housed. My friend Julie does the same. Like us, she has a younger son who isn't autistic, and he will be in Griffin's classroom.

Julie and I see each other more often, and our friendship grows. She tells me the story of how the pediatric neurologist told her and her husband that their son might never talk or do things other children learn to do. She tells the story of how another doctor told her he needed to be sedated with Depakote for his seizures. How another told her he would never be okay. She tells me about the years she spent in a depression, how hopeless she felt, how removed from her son, who she'd been told didn't really know or care who she was anyway. She tells me how her second pregnancy wasn't expected, and how she spent that time terrified she'd made a mistake, how she didn't know what her life could ever be again.

I feel like crying. I feel so enraged. I want to go back with her and find those doctors. I want to ask them what they thought they were accomplishing by telling a young mother, a vulnerable woman in love with her child, desperately afraid of what was happening, that her child would never do certain things. I want to know why they thought it was a good idea to tell her such things when science doesn't know enough about autism to say them. I want to go back. I want to change this for all of us. I want to take back the things we lost, the time with our children, the nights that shouldn't have been spent wide-eyed and terrified. I want them back.

* * *

Visual Learning

When the school year starts, Michael and I gather our hope around us like blankets. We can't stop hoping. It's our child. At the open house, I take pictures and, using a self-publishing website, make Ezra a social story about attending his new school. It's so helpful that these resources exist, making it possible for me to create a personalized book with photos of him engaged in the activities he'll actually be doing at school. I'm aware that Ezra is growing up in a time when these sorts of tools, technologies that will serve him, are available to him.

The computer makes Ezra feel connected, real, attached to a world where one thing equals another, where the world is predictable and whole and sane. I can't imagine how different it must have been in the refrigerator-mother era of the mid-twentieth century, when mothers were blamed for their children's disabilities and put into therapy to learn how to love, while their children were put in homes where they received abusive therapies, such as electric shock treatments. I feel both grateful for the era Ezra was born into and sick with grief for the children who weren't so lucky.

Griffin is excited about going to school. I've talked to him about it a ton. We've practiced saying goodbye. I've reminded him his brother is right next door. The first morning, we drive the half hour to the school. Ezra says goodbye easily. He's used to this by now, I suppose. Plus, he knows the teacher, who during the summer spent some time with him and Julie's son, teaching them a few social skills.

Griffin begins clinging to my leg as we drop off Ezra. By the time we enter his room, he's crying.

"I'm shy!" he says as he sobs. This is what he says about himself lately, which seems like good self-awareness.

"You're going to have so much fun," I tell him. "You're so good at making friends. And I'll be here this afternoon to bring you and Ezra back home."

Gradually he's able to untangle himself from me and enter the room. The class is mostly boys. One says, "Want to play?"

Griffin has trouble meeting his eyes, but he nods his head and tentatively follows the boy to a play kitchen.

"I'm making pancakes," the boy says.

"With syrup?" Griffin asks.

"Yes."

I tell Griffin I'm leaving, and he barely looks at me. "Bye, Mommy," he says in a tone of voice that suggests I'm cramping his style.

On the way home that afternoon, I ask Ezra how his day was. He says nothing, just looks out the window, munching on cheese puffs.

"My day was good," Griffin says. "But it takes too long."

"What do you mean?" I ask.

"I don't like to sleep there." He starts crying. "I don't want to nap. You come get me sooner."

I reach back a hand and rub his leg, trying to soothe him. Amazing to have these conversations with my three-year-old, to know so much about what is in his heart. I'm both thankful and afraid—how much did I not know about Ezra? How much still goes unseen?

As the weeks pass, Griffin continues to express his concern about napping at school. When I talk with his teacher, I learn it's not really napping, it's his waking up there that he doesn't like. He and his brother both experience nap hangovers, where they wake up groggy and disoriented and grumpy. Feeling that way away from Mommy is extra rough. Griffin also has a lot of nightmares, like I did as a kid. My mother told me I didn't sleep through the night until I was seven. I remember that. I remember feeling scared every night, waking in my bed in a dark room, running to my parents' bed with its warmth and its comforting mommy and daddy smells. Even though I'm always sleep deprived, I go quickly to Griffin when he wakes up crying, because I remember so well. I keep him cuddled tightly against me for the rest of the night.

He is also overly cautious and nervous about other children and what they will think of him. He is frightened of water in his eyes when we wash his hair. We have to bribe him with chocolate to get him to let us do it, and then his screams suggest unbelievable terror. I tell him, "Honey, it's okay. You're fine. I promise to be careful."

Between sobs he says, "Okay, okay. I'll calm down. I'll do it." He talks himself down from immense fear the entire time. We

seven years old

have to hold him wrapped tightly in his towel when it's over so he can catch his breath.

Like Ezra, Griffin has feelings and behaviors and ways of being in the world that make life rougher than it needs to be. I wonder often why Ezra has to spend his entire childhood working to change those things but Griffin doesn't. Is it solely because Griffin speaks better than Ezra can?

Somewhere during this same period of time, Michael and I sit together after entertaining friends and acknowledge our relationship. We are separated. We don't sleep in the same bed. We haven't had sex in four years. We have not touched or kissed for close to that amount of time. We like each other. We love each other. But we are more like friends than we are a married couple. There is no blame or anger. We wonder whether this would have happened if it weren't for Ezra. We have to wonder this, which is painful for both of us. It's not really Ezra; it's us. We weren't good at moving toward each other when the fear and despair rose up. We turned away from each other at the worst time, and something essential was lost. For now, we don't make any plans beyond this conversation. No one moves out. So, there it is.

Like magic, an event for me to promote my book is scheduled in New York City. I call and tell Frank about both pieces of news— my conversation with Michael and my pending travel. We make a plan to meet up at my hotel while I'm there. So, there that is, too.

We meet in the hotel lobby and go straight to the room. No need to pretend this is anything else. We are finally going to be together. I'm officially free to do so. He isn't. But it seems like something we have to explore after all this time. In the room, we sit for a moment on the bed. It's awkward. Then he says, "Can I kiss you?" which is not at all how I wanted this to go. But I say yes, and we kiss. We move relatively quickly, stripping off our clothes. He is a gentle lover, and he orgasms quickly. I do not. Afterward, we put our clothes back on and go out for something to eat.

I try to figure out how I feel, but can't seem to. Mostly, I feel detached from what is happening, as if I'm watching someone else's life movie. We talk like we always do about what other plans we have in the city and what we hope to do if there's enough time. Then we head back to the hotel for the night. The weather is crisp, the city busy with its usual hustle. We walk side by side. I glance over often, trying to decide if I'm still attracted to him. It occurs to me that this evening would have been so much more exciting had it happened back before I was married, when my faith in romantic love and passion looked different, when I cared more about that than anything else in the world. Basically, I wish this could have happened before Ezra came along and turned my life into something else.

When Frank leaves the next morning, we hug goodbye. It is an affectionate hug. A friendly hug. Maybe, as with Michael's and my separation, I'm seeing everything clearly now, like a lens has focused. Maybe I'm seeing Frank and me for what we are: a fantasy. On the phone later, I tell him this. I tell him I'm done. I don't feel that we will be together.

seven years old

"So, what, after ten years we finally have sex and then you're done?"

"I can see how it looks like that," I say. I am pacing in the kitchen. The kids are at school, Michael at work. I should be writing.

"Pretty obviously," Frank says. He's pissed.

"We've been using each other for ten years," I say. "I guess I needed this to happen to see this truth more clearly."

"Well, sure, we've already determined that," he says. "But there is also real love here."

I don't say anything. I don't know that I agree. Our love was built almost solely on illusion. Just like how this world convinced me to imagine Ezra as not functional, as needing to be something other than he is. It's so hard to see Ezra honestly and accurately, and yet it is my job to constantly try to.

"I'm sorry," I say finally, words so inadequate.

NOT LONG AFTER Ezra turns seven, Michael and I notice that something is going on with his vision. He stands to see the television. He peers and squints at objects that are far away. This is not completely surprising. Michael is nearsighted, as is everyone in my family except me. One of our children was bound to wind up with bad eyes. Ah, the eye doctor! I left that one off my list. As with the dentist, I should have taken him years ago to have his eyes checked. This is one more way we've done life differently than we might have. One more way we have felt paralyzed by the challenge of what for others is a basic aspect of parenting. I contact the director of Ezra's school for a recommendation, because her son wears glasses.

The doctor she recommends highly sounds like another Dr. Rogers. But his schedule is full until the fall because he is so popular, and we have to wait a few months for an appointment. Ezra starts a new school year. He grows taller. Time keeps moving. The week of the appointment, he wakes up with a stomach flu. At this point, we know what's coming. We know Ezra won't be back to health for a number of days. He will become thin and hollow eyed, but not dehydrated. He'll ask for milk and will refuse water. When we finally break down and let him have milk, he'll throw it up. One morning he'll wake up with a different sort of energy, or something will shift halfway through the day, and he'll start smiling and laughing and speaking again.

Many autistic kids act nonautistic when they have a fever. There's good scientific evidence that this is due to some muck-up in the neural pathways at the top of the spine and the cytokines produced by the immune system during fever. This doesn't happen to Ezra. Instead, he always goes silent, has trouble paying attention to anything outside of his internal misery, which seems more proof to me that he is atypically autistic. Perhaps someday, when they break autism down into many different categories, we will find he deserved a different diagnosis. Which is why when he starts nodding during this illness, I'm both surprised and pretty delighted. Ezra is seven and before now has never nodded in his

seven years old

life. He would shake his head early on, but nodding is something he has never picked up. Likely, he understands nodding now, and he really doesn't want to talk when he feels so bad, so he answers with nods instead of his usual, softly spoken yes. Ezra's new skill reminds me to be patient, to trust him. He will get there. He will learn things on his own terms.

Because he is sick, we have to put off the appointment and wait a few more months again. In those months, he has another developmental growth spurt. I pick him up from school, and when I ask, "Did you have fun at school, Ezra?" he says, "Yes."

"What did you learn today?"

"Reading."

"What else?"

"Music."

"Who is your favorite friend at school?"

A smile. "Ashley." Ashley is his teacher.

Once, I go to bring him home and he bounds toward me in the classroom. "I did art today!" he says.

Another morning, he walks into the kitchen, where bacon cooks. "What's that smell?" he asks.

Pointing at the sky one night toward the flashing lights of an airplane moving and blinking, "What is it?"

In the car, carrying the M&M's he wants to play with but not eat: "I want to show Daddy."

Something has clicked. Something in his brain has taken

another silent step forward. And as with every other time this has happened, another realm of development has opened up. He wipes himself appropriately after using the toilet, flushes it down, and washes his hands without being told. He buckles his own seat belt without being asked. They grow. They do. It's so easy to forget, Julie and I note to each other. So easy to be lost in the grief and comparisons and all the "he'll nevers" we were told about.

Ezra begins new projects. He makes videos on the computer. He names one *The Untabels*. I have no idea what that means, but I love watching the video, which includes his saying, "The world places to the map!" and then shows a map of the world. He says, "San Francisco to Logo!" and from a dot that marks San Francisco, a line travels to some distant place named Logo. I watch it again and again, laughing, my eyes tearing. We make another video together, called *The ABC Song*. He says, "Ladies and gentlemen, here's Ezra and Mommy!" and then we sing the song. Later he goes back in to do a voice-over so he can sing other parts of the song over us, making it more interesting. He's proud of these videos. When we watch them, or when I show them to other people, he looks to see their reaction. He wants to know what they think.

He finds a video on my computer of Griffin wiggling his hips and singing, "I'm shaking my body, shaking my body." He follows poor Griffin around the house, saying, "Shaking my body, shaking my body," standing in Griffin's path, trying to connect with him in this way. Griffin is annoyed. He cries, "I don't want to shake my body, Dezwa!" But sometimes he warms to Ezra's attention, and he and Ezra sing it together. They run around the house together singing.

Sometimes, Griffin says sentences using Ezra's cadence: "Want a treat." "Want some juice."

Once, he overhears me telling someone Ezra is autistic. He says, "No, *I'm* autistic."

"No, honey," I tell him. "You aren't. Ezra is."

"I'm autistic too!"

"You're not, baby."

Griffin cries and runs out of the room. "I am too!" he yells.

At school Ezra loves art and music. He sings Queen's "Bohemian Rhapsody" from start to finish, knows all the songs from *The Lion King,* and earns a solo in the Christmas pageant his school will perform. He dances and likes the tire swing. He knows who our first president was, and he knows the name of our current one. He knows that the White House is in Washington, D.C., and that the Golden Gate Bridge is in San Francisco. He does not, however, eat. Still. His eating stays stuck, as though caught in a grate.

His teachers make him drink water and eat bananas and fruit leather before he is able to do what he wants, usually time on the computer or for someone to sing a song to him. A few times I've arrived to see him with half a banana in his hand, or a quarter of a fruit leather left, his teacher encouraging him to continue, his expression twisted with anxiety and disgust. His teachers smile widely at me, as if to say,

Look how great he's doing! I smile back, say, "Wow, yes, that's wonderful." But inside I wonder how he will survive with this eating disorder of his, how he will ever eat enough food to live healthily and well. It is not useful to think this way. There's nothing that can be done, certainly nothing more than what is being done. We have to let his brain's tight hold over his eating loosen when it's ready to do so, which may be in a year, which may be never.

Sometimes I feel like the things I hope for are never right. When he is upset he pretends to fall down, says, "Whoa! Whoa!" and, once he's on the floor, says, "Are you okay, little buddy?" He says, "Did you bonk your head?" and holds it. But he hasn't bonked his head. He's upset about something but can't tell me what it is. He cries and cries, says, "I want to feel better!" but no matter how I ask in so many different ways, he can't tell me what the problem is. Later, I discover the wireless connection on his computer was out, or Griffin took something he wanted, or he wants to see his father, or I never find out. It will resolve itself on its own and I'll be confused, helpless, and wondering once more how I can ever be a good mother to my son. He can talk, yes. He can answer yes and no questions. He can wipe himself appropriately now after using the toilet. But he's still at a loss when it comes to his needs' being met on a deeper level. He's still disconnected from us in some essential ways.

One afternoon, Griffin asks me if I think Ezra would like some of his gummy bears, which are also vitamins. I know he won't, of course, but I say, "Why don't you ask him?"

seven years old

I follow little Griffin down the stairs to where his brother is playing Wii Music in the family room.

"Dezwa," Griffin says. "You want some of my gummies?"

Ezra ignores him.

"Dezwa! You want some of my gummies?"

Still nothing.

Griffin turns to me and says, "Sometimes Dezwa don't like to talk."

"That's true about him," I say.

Another day, talking about food, Griffin says to Michael, "Dezwa won't eat that, though."

"I bet you're right," Michael says. "Because what does Ezra eat?"

"Cheese puffs," Griffin says.

"And what else?"

"Cookies."

"And what else?"

"That's it."

Really, we should buy those damn Smart Puffs at wholesale prices. For a while I order them and the Earth's Best cookies in cases from Amazon. I have them set up on a delivery schedule to arrive once a month, which works well until our checking account dips under one month and Amazon cuts us off. We have a shelf in the pantry that is devoted to Ezra's food. The shelf is low enough that Ezra can reach the bags and boxes himself, and he does. He opens the drawer where he knows there are scissors, slices open the bags, and leaves the drawer open, the scissors on the counter, and the top of the bag on the floor.

Sometimes we actually run out of his food, which seems absurd considering all we have to do is keep enough of three items—cheese puffs, cookies, and milk—in the house for Ezra. But those times do happen. Like today, when Ezra emerges from his room and says, "Want some cheese puffs?" I realize there are no more. He has become picky lately and won't eat them when the bag isn't newly opened or if when we open the bag it rips, which is infuriating, because, well, is he not picky enough? As a result, he's been moving quickly through the bags. Michael is at work, which means it's up to me to buy more

"We have to go to the store," I tell him.

"Go to store to get cheese puffs?" he says.

"Let's go."

I put Ezra's clothes back on him because he took them off soon after we arrived home today; then I put shoes on both the boys. We drive to the store that usually has the cheese puffs we need, but of course they are out of stock. I tell the boys, warning them that we will have to get in the car again to go to the only other store in town that stocks them. A pediatrician I will never go back to once said to me, "Who let him have the cheese puffs in the first place?" I hated her at the time—such a cruel thing to say to me—but right now I agree. His rigidity around even the brand is exasperating. I didn't want him eating cheese puffs in the first

seven years old

place, but right now I see the fourteen other types of cheese puffs available and desperately wish he would eat them all.

In the next store, they have them: the purple-and-cream bag. I've never loved nor hated a food item more. Sometimes Michael will reach for an already opened bag on the counter and proceed to eat them while I stare at him, horrified.

"How could you eat those fucking things?" I ask.

Here in the store, both boys are in the cart, Ezra in the main basket where the food normally goes, Griffin in the seat kids are supposed to ride in. I put them in there so there will be no dilly-dallying, no calling them back to me. I pile every last bag of Smart Puffs I find on the shelf around Ezra while he smiles, thrilled to be surrounded by his favorite food. He pops one open as we ride up to the checkout counter and starts eating.

Times like this remind me of a potluck I attended once where one of the mothers poked around the food table, concerned because there was no brown rice, only basmati rice, and she only fed her three-year-old daughter only brown rice. I said something—oh, I couldn't help it, I had to—about how if my son ate even one grain of that evil basmati rice I'd be a happy woman. The woman proceeded to explain to me the detailed nutritional benefits of brown rice over those of basmati. I stood there, mouth open, desperate to move away from her.

THE DAY FINALLY arrives for Ezra's eye doctor appointment. I run late, as I always seem to do these days, so I must rush as I pick him up early from school. When I arrive, he's frustrated because he got water on his shirt while playing some sort of water game.

"New shirt!" he says.

"I don't have a change of clothes for you, Ezra," I say. "And we don't have time for anything else. You have to keep that on."

"Want a new shirt!" he says.

I sigh and impatiently take him by the hand to lead him to the car. The second he's in the car he starts removing his clothes—first the offending shirt, then his shoes and socks, his pants, and his underwear.

"Ezra, no," I yell, but he keeps going until everything is off.

Luckily it's a sunny day, so I lay his clothes across the empty car seats in the hope that they'll dry on the way to the eye doctor's office. I glance back to see him completely naked, the seat belt cutting into his white, fleshy tummy. He plays a game on his iTouch, which I brought to keep him occupied in case there's a long wait at the doctor's office.

When we arrive, his clothes are still damp, but I make him put them on anyway. He doesn't complain, which is a relief, and we head inside the building. In the waiting room, Ezra finds a plastic barn with some animals and starts to play while I check us in. There is another mother in the waiting area with her two children, one who flaps his arm and talks excitedly to her, then bounces off, his arms still flapping. I sit across from her, sensing the urge I always feel to connect in some way with a mother who also seems to have a child with special needs. I crave those moments, I realize, when another person and I can cross the vast spaces between us, when we can learn that we are really not all that different, that we aren't really alone. But I say nothing, and soon enough the assistant comes out and announces Ezra's name.

She takes us into one of the examination rooms and tells Ezra to sit on the chair. He does and then looks at me and points to the array of mechanisms attached to the chair.

"Yes," I say. "Pretty cool, but don't touch."

The assistant notes that we are here because we think Ezra might be nearsighted, and I nod. She turns on a screen behind Ezra that reflects onto a mirror on the opposite wall.

"Can you read the top line, Ezra?" she asks, and she points to the mirror. Ezra turns around to see the screen, always more curious about how things work.

"No, the mirror, Ez," I tell him. I point to it, but because he isn't looking, I physically move his head so he'll look at the mirror. I never know exactly when to let people know about Ezra's autism, but it seems we've hit that point where she needs to know. "He's on the spectrum," I say.

"Yes," she replies. "That's fine."

I glance at Ezra, concerned lately about what that is like for him when I announce his neurology. I want him to feel comfortable with the idea that he's autistic, and I try to say it as nonchalantly as I can. Also, I want him to have that language himself someday, to understand why he thinks differently from a lot of other people, why he's different in the world. But I fear now that when I say it he'll think he's doing something wrong and that I'm excusing him.

Ezra still twists his body around, looking at the screen.

"Ezra," I say. "Look over here, at the mirror. Look at these letters. What does it say?"

He says a nonword formed by the letter sounds.

"Okay," she says, "what about the last line? What letters do you see?"

Ezra is becoming annoyed. I can feel his tension, how he shifts around in his seat. Whenever someone wants something from him that he doesn't understand, he becomes agitated like this.

"This line," I say. "What are the letters?"

He turns again to see it on the screen behind him, then back to the mirror. He says the nonword formed by those letter sounds.

"I think he can read them," I say, "based on the word he just said."

She agrees and takes us to the room where he has to rest his chin on the metal cup and receive a puff of air in his eye. We do one eye, but then Ezra doesn't want another puff, so we move on. She puts us in another room to wait for the doctor, who joins us soon afterward. Everything my friend told me is true. He's just like Dr. Rogers was, kind and patient. He talks to Ezra like any other kid, and he makes the exam as fun as he can. He lets Ezra use the lever to move his seat up and down, and he lets him play with the red and blue glasses after he's used them to learn something about Ezra's eyes.

seven years old

"Well," he says after he's spent some time examining Ezra's eyes, "he's not nearsighted."

"He isn't?"

"Nope. He has very healthy eyes. Everything looks good."

"Then why is he squinting so much?" I ask.

He explains that Ezra has a sensory-based condition, not uncommon in autistic children, where the muscles in his eyes don't work together at the right time. The squinting comes from his trying to focus, to make his eyes work together at the same time. Basically, the connection between the two eyes isn't strong enough, and Ezra needs to build up the muscle strength in his eyes. He tells me that Ezra needs therapy to integrate his visual sensory function. Meanwhile, eyeglasses can help him focus until he builds that strength.

I admit that I am just a little heavyhearted. He needs more therapy. Again. Of course, I'm thrilled he isn't nearsighted, but frankly, if he were merely nearsighted, we would wait until he was old enough and then have laser eye surgery to fix it. While every other kid in the world who squints winds up with nearsightedness as a diagnosis, my kid has to again suffer through more therapy to improve.

In the eyeglass station, a young woman tries different frames on Ezra's face. He just looks so damn cute with those glasses, so I take photo after photo on my phone and send them to Michael.

"Play with barn?" Ezra asks.

"Not yet," I have to keep telling him. "Soon. Almost done." Finally we find ones that look right on him.

I order his glasses, which cost $650 including the special prism frames that help him to integrate his eyes. Then I make the appointment for his sensory evaluation, where I will have to pay another $250.

On the way home I ask him, "Do you want to wear eyeglasses?"

"Yes."

That weekend, he and Griffin and I drive to visit Julie and her kids. We meet them at a park close to their house, a park with a dynamic water feature, disc swings, a large sandpit, and a rope-encased merry-go-round. I put the boys in their bathing suits and they run around the water fountain with the other two boys. Eventually, the other children move on to other activities. Ezra stays in the water. There is a tiny girl playing there, her mother close by. I hover, well aware that Ezra might be inappropriate with her: may try to hug her, lean down and smile in her face, say something like, "WiFi!" or even do something harmful without knowing it's harmful, such as pushing her down. Amazingly, he does none of these, even as the girl follows him around, wanting to be close.

An hour later, when all three of the other boys are ready to go home, Ezra spins on the merry-go-round with a gaggle of other children.

"Go faster!" he yells.

A few of the children look at him oddly, probably because of his robot voice, but they push the merry-go-round faster and say, "How's that?"

seven years old

Ezra laughs, always caught up in feeling his joy. I make him come down off the merry-go-round because it's time to leave. A few of the kids say, "Bye, Ezra," which means that someone asked him his name and he answered them clearly enough to be understood.

I never see anything coming with this guy.

Theory of Mind

If this were a different kind of special-needs-parenting memoir, I would find the therapy or supplement that would make Ezra all better. I would save him, or some doctor would. But that's not our story. The great feat in Ezra's and my story is that I do nothing. Finally, I do nothing. I let Ezra be who he is, and I let me be me, with all our limitations. I let Ezra show me that he doesn't need me to do anything but love him. I let him show me that I will be uncomfortable sometimes. I'll feel helpless. In our story, life doesn't suddenly become easy. Some days Ezra is joyful, or we all are. I believe he'll do something amazing with music someday, that he'll live on his own, or with a friend or a lover. That he'll make me look back at all my old worries and wish I hadn't wasted energy on them. Other days, I'm sure this won't happen. I'm wracked with that familiar grief. But that's just our lives together. There is no tragedy here.

One evening, the power goes out on our street. Griffin, who

has been in the family room watching TV, screams and cries, "Help! I'm scared of the dark!" I feel my way down the pitch-dark stairs as fast as I can, saying, "I'm coming, baby. Here I come. You're fine. Everything is fine." I go to him and hold his soft, sobbing body against mine.

I carry him upstairs with me, talking to him about how sometimes things can happen to the electricity source and the company has to come and fix it, which it will. He listens, holding me close. I set him on the kitchen chair and look for candles and flashlights. Ezra has been on his computer, which is battery-powered and surely still working, but the modem isn't, so I'm not surprised when he emerges from his room.

"Fix the lights?" he says.

"The power's out," I tell him, just like I told Griffin, I know already Ezra won't understand the way Griffin can. "The company has to fix it."

"Fix the lights?"

"There's nothing I can do, baby. The power went out."

He's distressed, pulling on me.

"Get batteries," he says.

I light some candles, look again for a flashlight. Griffin follows close behind me, unwilling to let me out of his sight. But when I come back to the kitchen, Ezra isn't there.

"Ezra?" I call.

"Dezwa?"

seven years old

Ezra's room is black, without even the usual sliver of light that angles in through the window from the street lamp.

"Ezra?"

I grope along the wall until I come upon his warm body in bed, hiding under the covers, hiding from the dark by joining it, I guess. Griffin and I climb into bed with him, and the three of us cuddle. I'm so aware in these moments how love is ineffable, how it's not a thing at all, just a sensation that moves between people. It needs no words, no sight, no hearing. I want Ezra and Griffin to know that they don't have to do anything to be loved. They don't have to be anything other than who they are. That no matter what happens, no matter what they do or say or become, I will always love them with every cell in my body. There is nothing they can do to change that. In the end, I'm pretty sure this is the only rule for parenting.

Reader's Guide

1. Why is this memoir titled *Seeing* Ezra? In what ways does the book examine the notion of seeing?

2. The memoir's subtitle includes the phrase: the meaning of normal. How does the book explore the meaning of normal?

3. Much of Kerry's memoir examines the experience of mother guilt. What do you make of mother guilt in your own life, and in your culture? How is it different and/or the same as Kerry's?

4. During one of the evaluations Ezra receives, Kerry notes that he "fails" again and again. Why do you think she uses this term? What does "failing" mean in this context?

5. Michael and Kerry decide not to limit Ezra's computer time. Why do they decide this? Do you agree or disagree with their decision and why?

6. At one point, Kerry says she thinks everyone needs therapy—not just those with diagnoses. Do you agree or disagree and why?

7. At times in her story, Kerry discusses grief. What do you make of her experience with grief? How does it affect her experience of parenting?

8. Kerry has what could be called an emotional affair. Do you judge her for this? Do you empathize?

9. Why do you think Michael and Kerry separate? Is autism to blame?

10. What do you make of the last line of the book?

Acknowledgments

THANKS TO BROOKE Warner at Seal, who saw the value in this project. Even more to Jueli Garfinkle, who helped me build a truer, more beautiful story, who took out all my "got"s and "though"s, made me define my antecedents, and just generally got it—I mean, understood my story. Special thanks to Merrik Bush-Pirkle for the work she did on the book, to Domini Dragoone for the beautiful cover and page design, and to Krissa Lagos for my "Fastest AQ Completion Ever" medal, which she may or may not have made during company time.

I cannot express adequately my family's gratitude to the people who have loved and respected Ezra over the years: Patti Hall, the talented speech therapist who restored my faith in practitioners who work with special-needs children; the entire staff at Victory Academy, but especially Ashley Hatchett, whose gifts surpass all expectations; Nadine Hamester, who watched after Ezra with the most tender care; and the many more who worked with Ezra briefly.

To my friends who know, especially Brittney Corrigan and Julie Swenson (I promised Julie that along with her other positive qualities, I'd mention that she has a great rack): Both would have been my friends even if we hadn't had in common the challenges and joys of loving our special-needs children.

To my extended family: on Michael's side, his lovely sisters and their partners, who were there for us in various ways, and the spectacular cousins who accepted and reached out to Ezra from the start (a special-shout out to Chelsea, who has made autism awareness one of her causes). And my parents and their partners, who have loved Ezra without reserve and have done whatever they could to support us and his growth and talents.

To Jim, Ava, and Atticus, who have taken Ezra into their hearts. To Michael, who will always be my family and best friend, and Griffin, whose love for his brother is beyond measure.

It is so very scary to write a book about your child, to risk not showing him accurately, to risk being misunderstood or having him be misunderstood. We take these risks with any memoir, but writing about my child took those feelings to a new level. Every last instinct I have as a mother is to protect him, to keep him safe, to keep him happy, and writing about him seems like a violation of that instinct in some ways. So thank you to all my readers who have come vulnerably to our story, and who have opened their minds and hearts to my son and to me.

About the Author

© HEATHER HAWKSFORD

KERRY COHEN is the author of *Loose Girl: A Memoir of Promiscuity*, *Dirty Little Secrets: Breaking the Silence on Teenage Girls and Promiscuity*, and the three young adult novels *It's Not You, It's Me;* *The Good Girl;* and *Easy*. She has appeared as a guest on *Dr. Phil*, the BBC, and WE Network's *The Secret Lives of Women*, as well as many others. Her essays have been featured in *The New York Times*, *The Washington Post*, *Brevity*, *McSweeney's*, and numerous other anthologies and journals. She lives in Portland, Oregon, with her family. Find out more at www.kerry-cohen.com.